NO FEAR Felting!

{ **Craft kits available now at the Maker Store!** }

T0373351

Enter promo code "NoFear" and receive a 20% discount on a craft kit of your choice, valid through September 30th.

http://store.makezine.com

Craft:
craftzine.com

Craft:
Volume 04

transforming traditional crafts™

Special Section
FANCY DRESS

Features

Columns

Vol. 04, July 2007. CRAFT (ISSN 1932-9121) is published 4 times a year by O'Reilly Media, Inc. in the months of January, April, July, and October. O'Reilly Media is located at 1005 Gravenstein Hwy. North, Sebastopol, CA 95472, (707) 827-7000. SUBSCRIPTIONS: Send all subscription requests to CRAFT, P.O. Box 17046, North Hollywood, CA 91615-9588 or subscribe online at craftzine.com/subscribe or via phone at (866) 368-5652 (U.S. and Canada), all other countries call (818) 487-2037. Subscriptions are available for $34.95 for 1 year (4 issues) in the United States; in Canada: $39.95 USD; all other countries: $49.95 USD. Application to Mail at Periodicals Postage Rates is Pending at Sebastopol, CA, and at additional mailing offices. POSTMASTER: Send address changes to CRAFT, P.O. Box 17046, North Hollywood, CA 91615-9588.

designalicious

beautiful things
to brighten
your day

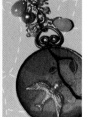

handcrafted jewelry
www.designalicious.com
designalicious.etsy.com

renga arts

cleverly crafted products from reclaimed & recycled materials

Main Street - Occidental, CA   **707.874.9407**
www.renga-arts.com   **info@renga-arts.com**

Craft:™ Projects

Make: SPECIAL EDITION

From the editors of
MAKE & CRAFT magazines

HALLOWEEN

» CRAZY CRAFTY COSTUMES! » MONSTROUS MAKEUP!
» FABULOUS FIENDISH FOOD! » HAUNTED HOUSE HOW-TOS!

SPECIAL EDITION ONLY $9.99!

LOOK FOR IT ON NEWSSTANDS SEPTEMBER 4TH!
PRE-ORDER YOURS IN THE MAKER STORE: STORE.MAKEZINE.COM

Craft:™ Volume 04

Crafter Profiles
Inside the lives and workshops of:

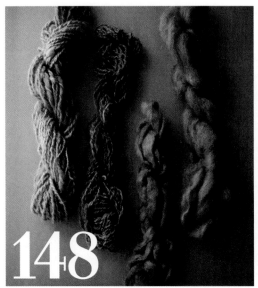

148

DIY

Make Cool Stuff

ON THE COVER
Our model, Angelica Amesquita, has her cautionary scarf adjusted by our creative director, Daniel Carter, and photo editor, Sam Murphy (on the left), while trusty photo assistant Ha Huynh (at right) does some assisting for Robyn Twomey, who photographed our cover on location at the former Navy base in Alameda, Calif.

Queenbee

Extra Arms

Rosie Ro

I'm Smitten

Sam Trout

See Kai Run

Clarity Miller

Tiny Meat

Sublime Stitching

buyolympia.com
Proudly showcasing the works of independent artists since 1999.

Sarah Utter

Nikki McClure

Arcana Soaps

Ivy Studio

Sherwood Press

Sara O'Leary

Puckish

Emily Ryan Lerner

Lucky Lilly

Jesse Reklaw

Jill Bliss

Little Otsu

Navigate with Care
Manatees are There

Boat Safely!

Save the Manatee® Club

www.savethemanatee.org

Photo © David R. Schrichte

Craft:
transforming traditional crafts™

EDITOR AND PUBLISHER
Dale Dougherty
dale@oreilly.com

EDITOR-IN-CHIEF
Carla Sinclair
carla@craftzine.com

CREATIVE DIRECTOR
Daniel Carter
dcarter@oreilly.com

MANAGING EDITOR
Shawn Connally
shawn@craftzine.com

DESIGNER
Katie Wilson

ASSOCIATE MANAGING EDITOR
Goli Mohammadi
goli@craftzine.com

PRODUCTION DESIGNER
Gerry Arrington

PHOTO EDITOR
Sam Murphy
smurphy@oreilly.com

ASSOCIATE EDITOR
Natalie Zee Drieu
nat@craftzine.com

COPY CHIEF
Keith Hammond

ASSOCIATE PUBLISHER
Dan Woods
dan@oreilly.com

ONLINE MANAGER
Terrie Miller

CIRCULATION DIRECTOR
Heather Harmon

STAFF EDITOR
Arwen O'Reilly

SALES & MARKETING ASSOCIATE
Katie Dougherty
katie@oreilly.com

CONTRIBUTING EDITOR
Phillip Torrone

MARKETING & EVENTS COORDINATOR
Rob Bullington

CRAFT TECHNICAL ADVISORY BOARD:
**Jill Bliss, Jenny Hart, Garth Johnson,
Leah Kramer, Alison Lewis, Matt Maranian,
Ulla-Maaria Mutanen, Kathreen Ricketson**

PUBLISHED BY O'REILLY MEDIA, INC.
**Tim O'Reilly, CEO
Laura Baldwin, COO**

Visit us online at craftzine.com
Comments may be sent to editor@craftzine.com

For advertising and sponsorship inquiries, contact:
Katie Dougherty, 707-827-7272, katie@oreilly.com

Customer Service cs@readerservices.craftzine.com
Manage your account online, including change of address at:
**craftzine.com/account
866-368-5652 toll-free in U.S. and Canada
818-487-2037, 5a.m.–5p.m., PDT**

Contributing Artists:
Melinda Beck, Scott Beale, Bill Cramer, Andrea DeHart,
Nick Dragotta, Margot Duane, Jason Forman,
Gabriela Hasbun, Tim Lillis, Robbyn Peck,
Beth Perkins, Jen Siska, Joe Szuecs, Robyn Twomey,
Robert Yeager

Contributing Writers:
Kent Bell, Joost Bonsen, Kris Bordessa, Gareth Branwyn,
Susie Bright, Annie Buckley, Christy Canida,
Andrea DeHart, Anna Dilemna, Joy Emery,
Victoria Everman, Diane Gilleland, Saul Griffith,
Christine Haynes, Brittanie Hoofard, Michelle Kempner,
Judith Lange, Matt Maranian, Anne McKnight,
Cathi Milligan, Brookelynn Morris, Moxie,
Ulla-Maaria Mutanen, Sally Myers, Helen Nodding,
Leah Peterson, Charles Platt, Angie Pontani, Jim Price,
Jean Railla, Racelle Rosett, Jenny Ryan, Peter Sheridan,
Eric Smillie, St!zo, Joe Szuecs, Kyle Thompson,
Tiffany Threadgould, Jason Torchinsky, Wendy Tremayne,
Lisa Viscardi, Betz White, Dora Reneé Wilkerson,
Megan Mansell Williams

Interns: Matthew Dalton (engr.), Adrienne Foreman (web),
Jake McKenzie (engr.), Lindsey North (crafts)

CRAFT is printed on recycled paper with
10% post-consumer waste and is acid-free.
Subscriber copies of CRAFT, Volume 04,
were shipped in recyclable plastic bags.

PLEASE NOTE: Technology, the laws, and limitations
imposed by manufacturers and content owners are constantly
changing. Thus, some of the projects described may not
work, may be inconsistent with current laws or user agree-
ments, or may damage or adversely affect some equipment.
  Your safety is your own responsibility, including proper
use of equipment and safety gear, and determining whether
you have adequate skill and experience. Power tools, electricity,
and other resources used for these projects are dangerous,
unless used properly and with adequate precautions, including safety gear. Some illustrative photos do not depict safety
precautions or equipment, in order to show the project
steps more clearly. These projects are not intended for
use by children.
  Use of the instructions and suggestions in CRAFT is at
your own risk. O'Reilly Media, Inc., disclaims all responsibility for any resulting damage, injury, or expense. It is your
responsibility to make sure that your activities comply with
applicable laws, including copyright.

Copyright © 2007 O'Reilly Media, Inc.
All rights reserved. Reproduction without permission is prohibited.
Printed in the USA by Schumann Printers, Inc.

Contributors

Michelle Kempner (*Knit Caution Tape*) is half tomboy, half craftster, which explains why her KitchenAid mixer and her laser cutter get equal placing in her heart. When she's not baking, she can be found watching movies, thinking about knitting internal organs, or playing touch football. Michelle lives in Brooklyn, N.Y., with her husband, James, and their two cats, Io and Milo. Michelle and James are partners in crime under the disguise Robot Clothes (robotclothes.com).

Susie Bright (*Susie's Home Ec*) takes time out of her busy schedule as a sex-radical anarchist to study sewing and fiber arts with her guru, Jill Sanders (heartgallery.com), who taught her everything she knows about needle and thread. Susie blogs about sex, politics, and dressmaking at Susie Bright's Journal (susiebright.com), and never gets tired of putting two right sides together.

Tim Lillis (*Project intro illustrations*) is a San Francisco-based illustrator, graphic designer, musician, and aspiring professional zombie actor. He frequently works with Kaiju Big Battel, the world's only live monster wrestling spectacle, and enjoys playing extreme bocce, applying wood grain to everything, and lighting things from below to see if there's anything that doesn't look creepy. Some of his work can be viewed at narwhalcreative.com, and some of his thoughts can be heard at continuityconcern.com.

A freelance writer who loves to craft, **Anna Dilemna** (*Not Your Grandpa's Embroidery*) is always on the lookout for the quirky side of life. She loves to travel and has lived all over the world, including New York, Chile, Paris, and Tokyo. Currently, Anna lives in Switzerland with her husband and 2-year-old son, and is excited about exploring the perfect balance between motherhood, feminism, and a crafty lifestyle. She can't quite decide whether her favorite tool is her seam ripper or garlic press. annadilemna.typepad.com

An evangelist for playing, **Judith Lange**'s (*101: Natural Dyeing*) all-time favorite question is "What happens if ...?" She believes this question is the key to opening doors that don't open otherwise. Her science background (pre-art school) and research lab work were perfect foundations for a lifetime of working experimentally. She's a fan of wheels (yarn spinning and pottery) because they have a mind of their own and are capable of making the most beautiful messes. Not a fan of pastels, Judy prefers colors that are mouth-watering. Her favorite tool is a sense of humor.

Beth Perkins' (*Burlesque Bouquet* photography) easygoing personality not only makes her job easier, but eases her subjects into making great photos. She's particularly fascinated with photographing factories and the people in them, and hopes to compile her collection someday. Beth was recently on assignment in Utah photographing salt miners and millers, and describes it as a photographer's dream. When she's not taking pictures, she's playing softball, taking surf trips with her husband, Keone, or eating pizza from Two Boots in Manhattan.

After years of watching various technologies become obsolete, **Joe Szuecs** (*Backyard Birdhouse*) moved from a hectic, high-tech life in San Francisco to the simple life in the small Sonoma County town of Occidental, Calif. Instead of long days in front of a computer screen, "Sooch" now creates functional art made from real-world reclaimed materials. Most likely because of his love of nature and animals, Joe began making modern, fully functional birdhouses. Joe also creates furniture, hypertufa planters and fountains, and other works.

Carla Sinclair
Welcome

>> Carla Sinclair is editor-in-chief of CRAFT magazine.
carla@craftzine.com

Fancy Dress

Reinvent yourself with fabric scraps,
repurposed clothing, and imagination.

Two years ago, my then-7-year-old daughter asked if she could have some lavender fabric that was left over from curtains we'd made. She said she wanted to make a dress out of it. "Sure," I said, not expecting more than a wraparound skirt knotted together at the corners. She hadn't yet learned to sew, so her dress-making tools were limited. I didn't give it another thought, until she emerged from her room an hour later in a long, sleeveless, mermaid-style dress that was hooked together in the front with gold pipe cleaners, each threaded through small "button-holes" that she'd cut with her kid scissors. Each pipe cleaner was then twisted into small flowers to secure the dress. I was truly amazed at how cool and inventive the outfit was.

> "*Fancy dress* can be traced to the Dark Ages, when it was popular for people to dress up as devils and saints."

Cut to last May, at the second annual Maker Faire in San Mateo, Calif., where over 40,000 people gathered to invent, create, and gawk at extraordinary projects that makers shared. Mixed in with the motorized cupcake cars, battling robots, and crafting demos was Swap-O-Rama-Rama, a bustling trading post (cost of entrance: a bag of used clothes) in which people of all ages swapped, cut, and remixed old clothes into amazing new garments — just as my daughter had done with her fabric. SORR's creator, CRAFT columnist Wendy Tremayne (*page 168*), told me she was impressed with all the clothing mods. "Silk blouses became transformed with ornate, artist-rendered silk-screen images. Ties became skirts and belts, and suit jackets were hacked by mixing other garments into them ... What's amazing about watching people make things at SORR is that people make clothing that is celebratory of their own personalities, rather than a compromise based on what's available on a rack in the store."

This notion of playful dress-up, self-expression through fashion design, and transformation of simple materials into something magical is the inspiration for this Fancy Dress issue of CRAFT.

Another term for costume, *fancy dress* can be traced to the Dark Ages, when it was popular for people to dress up as devils and saints (*page 46*), and has captured imaginations ever since, through masquerades, fancy dress balls, playing dress-up, and of course, Halloween.

We talked to some of our favorite costume junkies, including multimedia artist Marnie Weber, who uses thrift-store treasures and papier mâché to make spectacular costumes for all of her projects (*page 60*); hula hoop performer Annie Weinert, whose original costumes are as remarkable as her hoop dancing (*page 48*); and Angie Pontani, whose burlesque troupe relishes her handmade, awe-inspiring headdresses (*see page 50 to make one yourself!*). And if you'd like to expand your fancy dress horizons to include your canine companion, check out our DIY pirate pooch costume (*page 56*).

In addition to our fabulous Fancy Dress section, you'll find dozens of other crafty projects, including knitted caution tape, a suede macramé curtain, candy box purses, a crochet cocktail ring, a hay twine rug, a garden birdhouse, and much more. So grab your materials and your imagination, and bring it on. ✂

The best things really do come in small packages

But small objects can be very difficult to shoot, and you can end up spending big money trying to buy the right equipment. That's where these two little beauties come in. Packed with detailed instructions on how to capture the beauty of small, smaller and smallest objects, as well as tips, tricks and even a shopping list for building your own array of inexpensive photographic tools, these clever little books are creative and valuable resources for most any photographer.

rockynook

Look for these and other digital photography titles at your favorite bookstore or direct from O'Reilly at **www. oreilly.com/store**

Jean Railla
Modern Crafting

» Jean Railla is the author of the new domesticity manifesto *Get Crafty: Hip Home Ec* (Broadway Books). Obsessed with the craft of cooking, she is researching a book on underground food cultures.

Art vs. Craft

Sex, art, and rock 'n' roll was the motto of my early 20s. Free of any real responsibilities, I spent my youth at local rock shows or gyrating to Tropicalia records at living-room dance parties. When inspired, I would publish my handmade zine, or work on a video diary of my life in "the scene." Somehow, this fluid, artful existence felt organic to a time and place: Los Angeles in the years before hip became mainstream, Kurt killed himself, and MTV programming went reality.

At that moment, being an artist was about the culture of DIY — Do It Yourself. Its ethos, popularized by indie record labels like K Records, was simple: Don't like corporate rock? Start your own band. Disgusted by TV? Create your own shows. Think magazines are stupid? Xerox your own.

> The ultimate goal of the artist is to create more artists, to help others see themselves as more than just consumers.

While there are no retrospective museum shows documenting this DIY scene, and most of the musicians, performers, painters, and writers have disappeared from history, I see remnants of my old art-punk posse echoed throughout the modern crafting scene. The emphasis on being an individual, on carving a different path through the worlds of art and commerce, the sense of community both online and in cool craft fairs across the country, the culture of sharing, swapping, and working together in creative endeavors, are common to both movements.

The real difference between the old DIY scene and modern crafting might just be in size; crafting is now a $30 billion industry that has completely transformed how we look at knitting, crocheting, and all things domestic. Modern crafting is, in a word, huge.

Given this crafting renaissance, it seems odd that the art world seems to be distancing itself from the modern crafting movement. For example, New York City's Museum of Craft recently changed its name to the Museum of Arts and Design and launched the show "Radical Lace and Subversive Knitting," which featured a bevy of international artists using "crafts" in their artwork. Actual crafters were conspicuously absent. Where were Jenny Hart's portraits of rock legends like the White Stripes? What about Kathy Cano Murillo's Mexican-inspired shadow box art? Or an installation from the Church of Craft?

Maybe the problem with crafter "artists" in the eyes of curators is that they not only create, they also instruct others how to do the same. With the boundaries between art and craft breaking down, is this what separates us?

In 1934, social theorist Walter Benjamin proposed a new role for the artist that would help lead the way to a more progressive society: to create great works of art that, by design, would inspire others to do the same. Meaning that the ultimate goal of the artist is to create more artists, to help others see themselves as more than just consumers.

In this light, both the DIY scene and the modern crafting movement are on to something quite revolutionary. No matter how delusional and misdirected, my punk rock friends and I were transcending our roles as American consumers, and in doing so, we helped the movement spread. When Murillo shows others how to create their own shrines on her website, she breaks down the boundary between artist and audience — and inspires others.

At the end of the day, do I really give two crochet hooks about whether a quilt belongs in a museum or on a bed? No. What I, a proud crafter, really want to know is: *how did you make it?* ✕

I love your funky magazine. I like the eclectic mix of projects you feature ... kind of *Mother Earth News* meets *Cutting Edge*. Very cool. Finally, a magazine for those of us who wander the aisles at Lowe's and Hancock Fabrics with equal abandon.

—*Beth Bess*

Your article on fermenting wine in a plastic jug [*CRAFT, Volume 03, page 102*] is an interesting one, to say the least; however, I feel compelled to point out that your instructions ignore all modern sanitation practices. Fermenting any product at home poses a serious risk of botulism poisoning or other infection. By failing to include instructions for the proper methods of sterilizing fermentation equipment, you are putting your readership at risk of contracting a serious (and avoidable) illness. I think this calls for an addendum on your website and a correction in subsequent issues.

—*Jason Schreiber*

You raise a good question, Jason. We double-checked with a homebrew retailer, and with Linda Bisson, PhD, at the UC Davis Department of Viticulture and Enology. Both agreed that botulism generally is not an issue in winemaking because the bacterium *Clostridium botulinum* can't survive wine's high acidity (pH below about 5) or its alcohol content (above 7%). Black mulberry wine clocks in around 7% alcohol and a tart 3.5 pH.

However, "the caution against plastic is a good one," says Dr. Bisson. If plastic bottles are not thoroughly cleaned, a "biofilm" can build up over time, possibly providing a home for nasties such as *Salmonella*, *Staphylococcus*, or *E. coli*.

Our article advised readers to clean the vessel after fermenting and before drinking; we now also recommend a thorough cleaning and sterilizing *before* fermenting.

> "Finally, a magazine for those of us who wander the aisles at Lowe's and Hancock Fabrics with equal abandon."

> "I am now powerless to do anything else, including work, until I read every article and try as many of the projects as I can without leaving the house."

The three issues just arrived. I am now powerless to do anything else, including work, until I read every article and try as many of the projects as I can without leaving the house. This will surely lead to me being fired. Upside: I'll have more time for crafting when I'm unemployed. Seriously, thanks so much. I'm entranced!

—*Terri Stone*

Got my copy (subscriber!) today and am over the moon! I will have plenty to look at tonight. My husband brought in the mail, swiped it, and looked at it even before I could. Now the spine is all creased and the pages dented. :)

—*Rosemary Waits*

If you aren't familiar with our sister publication, MAKE, check us out online at makezine.com.

Got something to say? Write us at editor@craftzine.com

CALIFORNIA TABLE WINE, © 2007 CARLO ROSSI VINEYARDS, MODESTO, STANISLAUS CO., CA. ALL RIGHTS RESERVED.

LET THE JUG BE YOUR MUSE.

Inspiration can come from the most unlikely sources. Take the Cabernet Couch for instance. Made from 28 empty Carlo Rossi® jugs and simple hardwood, this deluxe divan was created as a part of the Carlo Rossi Jug Simple Furniture Collection. View the Cabernet Couch and the other pieces in the collection at **www.carlorossi.com**.

HANDMADE

Craft:
transforming traditional crafts™

Subscribe now to receive a full year of CRAFT (four quarterly issues) for just $34.95!*
You'll **save over 40%** off the newsstand price.

Name

Address

City   State

Zip/Postal Code   Country

Email Address

*$34.95 includes US delivery. Please add $5 for Canada and $15 for all other countries.

B7CTA

Order now to become a Craft subscriber!

craftzine.com/subscribe

craftzine.com

Order now to become a Craft subscriber!

craftzine.com/subscribe

Craft:
transforming traditional crafts™

Subscribe now to receive a full year of CRAFT (four quarterly issues) for just $34.95!*
You'll **save over 40%** off the newsstand price.

Name

Address

City   State

Zip/Postal Code   Country

Email Address

*$34.95 includes US delivery. Please add $5 for Canada and $15 for all other countries.

B7CBA

BUSINESS REPLY MAIL

FIRST-CLASS MAIL   PERMIT NO 865   NORTH HOLLYWOOD CA

POSTAGE WILL BE PAID BY ADDRESSEE

NO POSTAGE
NECESSARY
IF MAILED
IN THE
UNITED STATES

Craft:

PO BOX 17046
NORTH HOLLYWOOD CA 91615-9588

BUSINESS REPLY MAIL

FIRST-CLASS MAIL   PERMIT NO 865   NORTH HOLLYWOOD CA

POSTAGE WILL BE PAID BY ADDRESSEE

NO POSTAGE
NECESSARY
IF MAILED
IN THE
UNITED STATES

Craft:

PO BOX 17046
NORTH HOLLYWOOD CA 91615-9588

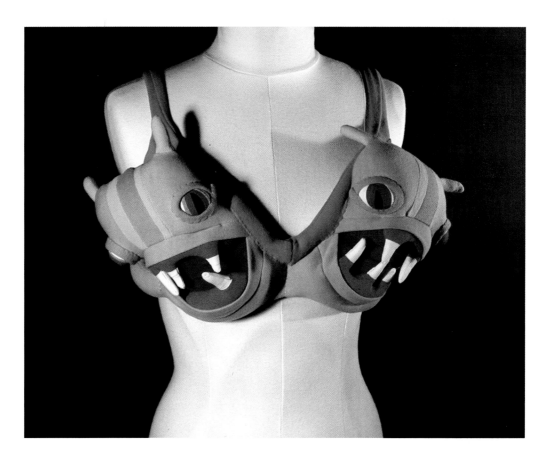

Monster Madness

Monsters haunt **Jennifer Strunge**. They lurk in every room of her home. Their bulging eyes stare from shelves. Their long, gangly arms reach out from every corner. They crowd her bedroom.

They even haunt her dreams — and Strunge could not be happier. "I love monsters," says the 25-year-old artist from Baltimore, Md., whose handcrafted creatures are winning her an international following.

In wild and varying colors of vintage fabrics, made without patterns so that no two are ever alike, her monsters range from the size of a small doll to those big enough to eat a man.

"Monsters are awesome," she says. "They have the capacity to frighten or protect, depending on whose side they are on. My monsters aren't scary. Kids laugh at them."

Strunge (rhymes with sponge) discovered her passion while working on her fine art degree in 2004, fabricating dozens of monsters crawling out from beneath a bed. "The monsters got a great response, and people kept asking me to make more," she says.

But her hand-sewn creations aren't content skulking beneath beds. Strunge also created a bra with twin snaggle-toothed monster heads, a baroque dress with fabric ram's horns sprouting from the shoulders, and an octopus to wear on your head.

Her oversized pieces include multicolored squid-like mutants, a hot pink mega-monster, and snakes peppered with dozens of lips. Several have been used in the local children's puppet theater, where Strunge works when she's not producing monsters.

Strunge's home studio is piled high with fabric and monsters in various stages of construction. "I tend to work in a chaotic manner," she smiles. "I'll sit down to watch TV and be making eyeballs. There are always pins and needles in my bed."

She sells her monsters at craft shows across the United States, and her website attracts buyers from around the world. But Strunge admits: "These monsters are like my babies. I spend so much time with each one in the making, sometimes it's hard to give them up." —*Peter Sheridan*

>> **Cotton Monster:** cottonmonster.com

Photography by Jennifer Strunge

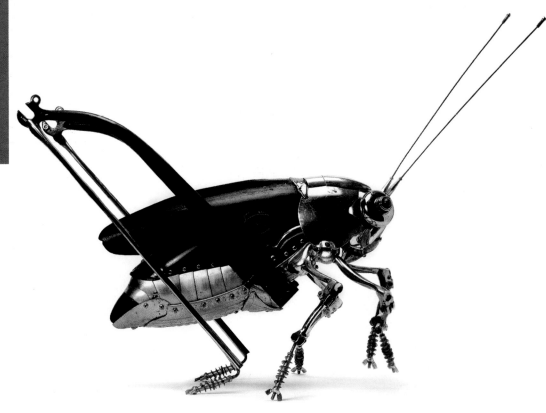

Junk Menagerie

No one could be blamed for looking too closely at **Edouard Martinet**'s stunning assemblage sculptures. What seem at first to be perfectly welded birds and bees, frogs and fish, are actually carefully crafted from found scraps and junk parts, with nary a solder or a weld. The realism is astonishing, particularly as you begin to realize that the elegant fins on a fish are actually metal spatulas and the gills are spoons. Martinet's juxtapositions are inspired; you'll never look at your trash in quite the same way again.

While his love of insects started with a childhood teacher who was an entomologist, it wasn't until he studied art in Paris during the 1980s that his interests collided. Martinet, who started his career as a graphic designer and moved into sculpture in the 90s, is now an artist and art teacher. He lives in Rennes, the capital of Brittany in western France, and is a regular at flea markets, car parts suppliers, garage sales, and second-hand stores. (And of course, now that the word is out, friends, friends of friends, neighbors, and family all call him on a regular basis: "When they get rid of their old things, they think of me.")

Each piece takes about a month to complete, although he often has two or three going at once. Sometimes he has a vision in his head when he starts, and he looks for parts to fit; other times, he takes a pile of gizmos and lets the objects themselves suggest his subject.

"The phobic animals are my principal sources of inspiration," Martinet says, meaning spiders, toads, wasps, and other insects. "And the animals which seem to be foolish or stupid, such as ostriches [or] fish, and I try to make them friendly, funny."

These transformations are not always understood at the source, though. "I often hide the real use of the bits and pieces I buy," he says, "because the sellers wouldn't sell them to me. For them, the car parts they sell have to be used to restore cars, and that's it. It sounds crazy to them to use these to make sculptures." —*Arwen O'Reilly*

≫ **Scrap Sculptures: edouardmartinet.com**

Photograph courtesy Edouard Martinet

Photograph by Cathy Kasdan

Plastic Age Style

At first glance, you'd think these dresses were costumes from an old Doris Day movie. In actuality, you're looking at hundreds of plastic bags.

These two 1950s-style outfits were hand-knit by **Cathy Kasdan**, a full-time art teacher and master's student in textiles at Kent State University in Ohio. She explored the theme of consumer culture for her final thesis by using plastic grocery bags as her medium for knitting. The stunning results make up Kasdan's *Transforming Consumer Culture* ensemble.

"The 1950s homemaker outfit and blue *Haute Culture* dress hearken back to a society that embraced the Plastic Age without reservation for the possible ramifications of consumerism," Kasdan explains.

A knitter for only two years, she's drawn to reusing materials; she started the project with her own plastic bag stash saved from trips to the grocery store.

"I've always looked for interesting materials and methods for expression, following the same guidelines of using available resources," Kasdan says. Once word of her project spread, she ended up receiving thousands of bags from friends and acquaintances.

Kasdan spent five months working on the 1950s outfit, using almost 400 bags. The blue haute couture dress took two months and 200 bags. Kasdan knit not only the dresses, but also all the coordinating accessories, including a pillbox hat, flower hat, purses, and accompanying shawl.

Using plastic bags as yarn definitely had its difficult moments. "The bags' lightweight and static nature were the main challenges," says Kasdan. "Trying to cut an entire bag into one continuous strip while it's floating up or sticking to itself can take a long time. Some evenings I spent hours just cutting the bags. I found that knitting a single layer of plastic worked better for me than doubling up the layers by attaching loops made of bags to each other."

Research suggests that 500 billion to 1 trillion plastic bags are consumed worldwide each year. Kasdan's plastic ensemble brings to light the notion that innovations of the past don't always end up being progress today.　　—*Natalie Zee Drieu*

≫**1950s Plastic:** flickr.com/photos/cathykasdan

Photography courtesy of David Mach and Cass Sculpture Foundation, www.sculpture.org.uk

50-Point Bonus

Like many crafters, **David Mach**, an art-degreed, professional sculptor, has a deep obsession with repurposing everyday stuff. He's created major works out of wire coat hangers, safety matches, and old magazines, exploring the tension between high-brow art and quotidian, throwaway materials. He once built a life-sized nuclear submarine out of castoff car tires. His coat hanger sculptures must be seen to be believed, and you'll be amazed at the curves he coaxes from square Scrabble tiles in his nine-foot-tall nude, *Myslexic*.

Though they seemingly sprang to life from a colossal junk drawer, Mach's sculptures are anything but thrown together. "They're made traditionally," he explains, "first modeled in clay, molded, then cast in Scrabble pieces, dominoes, and such."

Isn't that a huge pain in the neck? "I have an excellent assistant, Patrick Milne, who actually glued all of the Scrabble pieces together in the mold." It pays to be boss.

Mach made his name in the 1980s with his art installations in which massive objects — pianos,

cement mixers, cars and trucks — are engulfed in voluptuous waves of old magazines and newspapers.

Of his latest series of oversized nudes, Mach says, "All of the figures get a good reaction from the public, who are amazed that it's possible to use such materials to make art."

When he's not rollerblading, skiing, or windsurfing, Mach can be found in his southeast London studio working on new sculptures, extravagant photo-collages (all those leftover magazines), and proposals for public artworks around Europe.

He recently was named Professor of Inspiration and Discovery ("a newly created position and a helluva title") at Dundee University in his native Scotland, where he has proposed a huge female figure leaning casually over a campus science building, like a dean keeping an eye on her scholars. A 60-foot-tall nude dean, made of an everyday material to be announced.

—*Keith Hammond*

≫ **Scrabble Nude:** davidmach.com

Decked Out

If elegant accessories made from banged-up skateboards sound impossible, think again. **Rebecca Hickey** turns trash into shredder fashion with her successful, eco-friendly company, Beck(y). The 36-year-old Long Island native (half her friends call her Beck, the other half Becky) is no poser. She used a skateboard to get around when she was living in Minneapolis after college. Now, decks are her muses.

The idea to turn boards into bags came three years ago on a shopping excursion in SoHo. At Prada's flagship store, a sleek modern space designed by Rem Koolhaas, Hickey noted a giant, zebrawood curve called "the big wave" running through the building. She saw a half-pipe. "I wondered if anyone had ever broken in and tried to skate it," she says.

Admiring the retailer's bejeweled, satin-lined purses, Hickey dreamt up a combination of fine fabrics and skuzzy skate gear. She got an old deck from the owner of 5boro Skateboards and sewed some satin lining. She cut the deck with a chop saw, smoothed the edges, then fixed wood to satin with industrial glue. Although she removed the grip tape and street crud, Hickey left the graphics and scrapes intact. "Skateboards are so personal to their owners," she says. "The stickers and scratches tell the story of what that board has been through. I try to keep it as authentic to that as I can."

Hickey has made some 4,500 "Sk8bags" by hand in her Upper Manhattan live-work space. From dynamic totes to colorful clutches, her collection, which also includes gym bags, belt buckles, iPod cases, and money clips, is found in boutiques and galleries throughout the nation — even on the red carpet. And used decks keep pouring in. To give back, Hickey founded the Boards 4 Bowls program: working with groups including the Tony Hawk Foundation (the icon's wife has several Beck(y) bags), she donates $3 toward building public skateparks for every board she receives. Now that's rad.

—*Megan Mansell Williams*

≫ **Beck(y) Bags:** beckycity.com

Photography by Rebecca Hickey

OUR FAVORITE
TRINKETS & TREASURES

1

2

1. Dress Up

While not exactly play clothes, Jennifer Collier's artwork is a great reminder of the way clothes get loaded down with meaning. Her paper garments (made from old letters, vintage maps, and even dress patterns themselves) are a nod to classic little-girl dresses of years past and the dainty shoes are as delicate as Cinderella's.
jennifercollier.co.uk

2. Sew Real

The felted creations of Blythe Church always require a second look: is that sewing machine/camera/typewriter/whatever else she's working on really made from fabric? The intricacy (the sewing machine is threaded with real thread) and sense of humor (she even loaded film into the back of her felt Olympus SLR) are an inspiration, no matter what you craft.
sewnbyblythe.com

3. Can You Handle It?

Finally someone came up with a solution to the whole problem of cast-iron pot handles being hot and potholders not always protecting hands. These cozies are super cute and unbelievably functional! craftzine.com/go/pothandle

4. Tea and Sympathy

For those who've always felt that champagne is the tea of wines (oh so ladylike), these wonderful champagne cups are for you. Made by Hrafnkell Birgisson (try saying that 3 times fast), they are an excuse to drink sparkling wine regularly. hrafnkell.com

5. Feltalicious

Whether it's the green sheen perfectly captured on a blackbird's wing, or the choice of driftwood to create the head of a coyote, Jane Hirschman's creations are breathtaking, eerie, and exquisite. (And don't miss the photos of Ursa the felting dog.) mamaqilla.com

6. A Cut Above

Peter Callesen's amazing fantasy worlds allow us to see how they were made, like this archway that opens onto the very page it was cut from. He plays with the border between two- and three-dimensional space, and creates a surprisingly sturdy magic from the fragility of white paper.
petercallesen.com

7. Makin' Bacon

Regina Gonzalez makes fantastic patterns for things we never thought we'd want to knit. (The bacon wrap is especiallly fabulous.) You have to smile, or at least giggle nervously.
monstercrochet.
com/Patterns.html

8. A Stitch in Time

Claire Coles loves to stitch, whether a delicate edge or a messy scrawl. She sews elegant roses, cheeky birds, and scribbly branches on teacups, tables, and wallpaper, reminding us that embroidery isn't always contained within the hoop.
clairecolesdesign.
co.uk

Photograph of Peter Callesen installation courtesy of Emily Tsingou Gallery

9. Purple Rain

This knitted cloud takes the gloom out of a rainy day. It's simple but utterly charming and would be perfect for a mobile hanging over a baby crib (or heck, anywhere).

craftzine.com/go/rainycloud

10. Viva Mexico

If you've ever fallen in love with traditional Oaxacan embroidery but didn't quite feel it was you, the Mexican Dress Lady has a suggestion for you: make your own! She has beautiful examples of embroidery on her site, from both traditional patterns and her own.

themexicandress.com

11. Textile Jewelry

Becky Klay takes a good idea and makes it wonderful. Her detailed textile jewelry is modern with a wink to traditional embroidery. The eccentric shapes and colors reference everything from abstract art to nature.

smallmotordesigns.com

SOUTHERN ACCENTS

BY LISA VISCARDI

Shari Enge brings art and mystery to the craft of doll making.

★ Sara Jane has soul. An old Southern soul. You can see it in her mismatched button eyes, you can touch it in her flattened nail nose. You can even smell it in her taut muslin skin, which has the curious aroma of baked coffee. That sense of the Old South and a life lived long ago comes with the territory when you're a creation of Los Angeles doll maker Shari Enge.

"My great-grandfather was born a slave and fought in the Civil War," says Enge. "My father never liked to talk much about his childhood, so the South has always been a mystery to me. I like to think that sense of mystery and wonder, that longing to know the unknown about my family and the South, shows through in my dolls."

> "I like to think that sense of mystery and wonder, that longing to know the unknown about my family and the South, shows through in my dolls."

As the artist behind an ever-expanding line of handcrafted dolls, Enge's approach to doll making has a history as well: her own. "A lot of materials I use, and the process, are not that different from when I made dolls as a kid." After tracing a simple shape onto muslin, Enge sews it, stuffs it with fiberfill, stains it with coffee, bakes it, and then needle-sculpts its face. Vintage materials — some bought, some found — add to the distinctly Southern Gothic charm of her dolls. She uses lost keys, rusted wire, and even nails to adorn them. "The nails make incredible hair and noses. The older they are, the more worn they are, the better."

Having been a doll lover and maker her whole life, Enge felt compelled to turn her passion into a business, starting the Old Soul Doll Company in 2005. But it wasn't easy. "I didn't know if the dolls, or if I, were good enough." Early praise from friends and family had the ironic effect of making her more insecure. She feared they were telling her what they thought she wanted to hear. Enge got the truth at her younger daughter's Cinco de Mayo school fair, where she set up a booth. "So many people that I didn't know bought dolls from me that it gave me the confidence. I thought, 'Yeah, they *are* good!'"

Now happily settled in a home studio built by her husband, Scott, Enge's doll business is growing. Enge and her dolls were invited to be part of the Ten Women collective in Venice, Calif. She's also been featured on Joan Quinn's cable television show and is sparking the interest of galleries.

Yes, her business moves forward, but Enge never forgets to look back. "In a way, each time I make a doll, I make a trip back to my past. Sometimes way back, back before I was even born. The Old Soul Doll Company was born out of a need to connect to family." ✕

➕ See more of Enge's work at oldsouldollco.com.

Lisa Viscardi is a creative entrepreneur living in Santa Monica, Calif.

Photography by Robyn Twomey

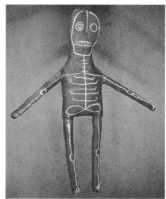

⭐ TOP: The faces of Southern charm (clockwise from top left): Virginia, Matty, Charlie, Memphis, Jean Michele, Murna. BOTTOM: Shari Enge in her studio.

THE LOST IPU ART OF NI'IHAU

BY KRIS BORDESSA

Michael Harburg and Bill Wright rediscover an ancient island craft.

When Captain James Cook sailed to the island of Ni'ihau in the late 1700s, he noted that the natives' household equipment was limited to "a few gourds and wooden bowls." The residents of Ni'ihau used hardshell gourds to carry liquids. Artifacts discovered on the island show that these gourds, or ipu, were beautiful as well as functional. Geometric patterns adorned the gourds in deep chocolate hues; the artistry on each melded with its background as neatly as a man tattooed.

With the influx of people to Hawaii in the 19th and 20th centuries, Western crockery replaced native vessels, and the art of gourd decoration became obsolete. The Ni'ihau artists who had handcrafted those gorgeous ipu took their secrets to the grave.

> While most gourds of this era were dyed from the outside, Chrisman discovered that the Ni'ihau gourds were dyed from the inside out.

But today, in the petite hill town of Holualoa on Hawaii's Big Island, artists Michael Harburg and William A. Wright work amid glossy dried gourds, creating ipu art with a technique re-created 17 years ago by a doctor named Bruce Ka'imiloa Chrisman. Chrisman had researched the vessels to figure out how they were made, re-creating a dye method similar to what he believed the ancient Hawaiians used. While most gourds of this era were dyed from the outside, Chrisman discovered that the Ni'ihau gourds were dyed from the inside out.

"Michael learned about the method from Bruce Chrisman, and started carving gourds as a hobby," says Wright. When Wright saw Harburg playing around with this method, he was inspired to try it himself, and quickly added carved ipu pieces to his repertoire. Eventually, the two partnered in developing the Ipu Hale Gallery.

Harburg and Wright use Chrisman's method and modern tools to remove the skin from green gourds, leaving behind geometric patterns and island scenes. When an image is complete, they fill the gourd with thick black coffee — the seeds and pulp still intact — and allow the gourd to sit for several weeks. The uncarved areas, still green, draw the dark color of the coffee out into the skin through capillary action. The carved areas remain light in color. Then the dyed gourds are emptied, cleaned, dried, and sealed to last a lifetime.

"Every gourd is different," says Wright. "Each one absorbs the dye a little differently, so some have a softer look, while others are very bold."

Both men are happy to talk about their art with those who visit Ipu Hale. But there's one group of people that Harburg would particularly like to share the process with. "Someday, I'd love to take what I've learned to the people of Ni'ihau, to bring it full circle." ✕

Kris Bordessa uses found objects and recycled items for most of the projects in her books, the latest of which is *Great Colonial America Projects You Can Build Yourself*. krisbordessa.com

Photography by Robbyn Peck

★ **MEN AT WORK:** Michael Harburg (left) and Bill Wright work amid glossy dried gourds, creating ipu art.

TRY YOUR HAND AT GOURD DYEING
using Harburg and Wright's technique.

1. Get to know your gourd. What shape of opening will it have? A large opening or a small one? Will it have a single focal point, or will it work best with a geometrical design that completely encircles the gourd?

2. Draw the pattern. Mark a line indicating where you will eventually cut the opening in the gourd. Sketch the pattern in pencil on the outside of the gourd, then finalize it using the permanent marker.

3. Cut in the design. With the X-Acto knife, outline the edges of the pattern. In areas that you want to be lighter in color, carefully remove a thin layer of the gourd's skin. Leave the green skin intact where you want the gourd to be darker.

4. Make the opening. With the pattern complete, use the X-Acto knife to cut a starter hole on the line that you marked for the opening. Slide the keyhole saw or jigsaw blade into the starter hole and, following the line you've drawn, cut the opening. *Do not remove the seeds or pulp from inside the gourd.*

5. Dye the gourd. Pour the strong coffee into the gourd and set the project aside in a cool, dry place for about 3 weeks.
NOTE: This stage can get a little smelly.

6. Dry the gourd. Pour the coffee out and remove as much of the wet fiber as possible. Scrape away all of the remaining skin; underneath is the dyed shell. Set the gourd aside until the shell is completely dry and hard. This may take 7–10 days, depending on your climate.

7. Finish the gourd. With the wire brush, clean any remaining pulp from inside the gourd. Use sandpaper to smooth the outside of the gourd. Seal the gourd, inside and out, with tung oil.

➕ More on Ipu:
Ipu in the collection of the Bishop Museum
   on Oahu: craftzine.com/go/oahuipu
Hawaii Gourd Society: outtayourgourd.net

Materials

» **Green, hard-shell bottle gourd**
   (family *Cucurbitaceae*, species *Lagenaria siceraria* or similar) seeds available at many garden centers
» **Pencil**
» **Permanent marker**
» **X-Acto knife**
» **Keyhole saw or jigsaw**
» **Strongly brewed coffee,** enough to fill the gourd
» **Fine sandpaper**
» **Wire brush**
» **Tung oil**

Ulla-Maaria Mutanen
Linkages

Ulla-Maaria Mutanen is CEO of Social Objects, Ltd., founder of Thinglink (thinglink.org), and author of the HobbyPrincess blog (hobbyprincess.com). ulla@hobbyprincess.com

Pattern Recognition

Have you ever heard of cosplay? Combining the words costume and play, cosplay is a subculture that originated in Japan. (*Check out our article on page 54.*)

Cosplayers dress up as characters from comics and video games. I got the opportunity to attend my first cosplay party not too long ago. Feeling like Alice in Wonderland, I mingled among the hundreds of Super Dollfies, Elegant Gothic Aristocrats, and Loli-Goths, all wearing wonderful self-made or self-designed costumes. Trailing the global success of manga comics and anime cartoons, cosplay has made crafting costumes a growing trend worldwide.

Because more people are making their own clothes and accessories, the demand for useful blueprints and recipes is on the rise. Crafters, if anyone, should know that good patterns are valuable because they require hours of careful planning and design to create. Not everyone can express a complicated model in a simple way; those who excel at it can become celebrities. When Toronto-based crafter Jordy Lucier published an illustrated how-to for making a purse on craftster.org, the response was awe-inspiring. Hundreds of thousands of people viewed the instructions, and the post generated more than 100 pages of comments.

Virtual worlds, blogs, online communities, and discussion forums offer new channels for crowdsourcing patterns and recipes. They are changing the way patterns are sought out and distributed. For example, if you are a fan of the fantasy role-playing game *Dark Age of Camelot* looking for the sewing pattern of a Sepiroth jacket, you'll be happy to know one can be found on forums.cosplay.com. Thus, not only is the pattern itself valuable, but so is the knowledge of where to find it.

A freely editable pattern invites us to play and contribute. Patterns can be a puzzle. For example, showstudio.com has a neat downloads section where it publishes the patterns of legendary but extremely complicated fashion items, like the Alexander McQueen kimono jacket. In exchange for giving out the pattern for free, ShowStudio asks those who succeed in making the garment to send in photos of the result for publication.

The distribution of patterns in magazines has traditionally been a profitable business. But if that's the case, then why is Nicola Enrico Stäubli, a Swiss-based architect, giving away the patterns for his Foldschool cardboard furniture on the web for free?

One answer is that sharing free patterns generates goodwill. In a world where everybody wants to earn a nickel, giving out something for free makes you stand out from the crowd.

A freely editable pattern invites us to play and contribute.

Good patterns are sometimes referred to as the "source code" of great crafting. BurdaStyle, a spin-off project of Hubert Burda Media, pushes the software vocabulary even further. Burda has launched the concept of open source sewing, and offers a free pattern database for crafters around the world. A pattern can be freely downloaded and used as the base for other designs. During its first four months, Burda reports the database had more than 60,000 downloads in the United States.

Not all software programmers want to share their code. Likewise, many crafters consider good patterns their business secrets. Still, there are a growing number who believe that sharing patterns for free will eventually benefit the distributor and, in one way or another, generate a return on the investment. This makes sense. Who wouldn't like to have a passionate community promoting one's core business? ✄

ALBERT DeLOACH'S ENCHANTED FOREST

South of Austin, beside the railroad tracks, lies the Enchanted Forest. It was once a pig farm, then a hobo encampment, before it was transformed by **Albert DeLoach** (right) into a most unusual live/work space for artists and a unique outdoor performance venue. When DeLoach first bought the property 10 years ago, he started trucking out loads of rubbish, and working to restore the tree-lined limestone creek that ambles through the property.

He also had the help of others who got behind his vision to create an artist collective that now inhabits the forest. The Enchanted Forest now features Art Outside (artoutside.org) in the spring and the Haunted Trail (austinhauntedforest.com) in the fall.

Photography by Sam Murphy

BONUS FEATURE!

BRIDGE OVER ENCHANTED WATERS: This is the main bridge over the creek at the Enchanted Forest, which opens for evening concerts. At least twice a year, the bridge is washed away in a flood and a Forest crew must drag it back into place. Featured here is the work of Shrine, a collaboration of Los Angeles trash artists.

RECLAIMED HEART: Jack-of-all-trades Albert DeLoach's medium is trash.
His *Sacred Heart* is made out of metal recycled from washing machines.

FIRE PUPPET GYPSY: Resident artist **Baru**, short for Baruzuland, uses all sorts of found materials for her shadow puppets and other artwork. She is extremely prolific in modifying and beautifying everything in her space. She participates in what she calls "fire puppet gypsy theatrics."

MUSIC FOR THE MASSES: *Cranky*, a megaphone-music box art piece, brings together the frivolity of the circus and the elegance of the Victorian era. A large, interactive piece, it involves several people winding up the music boxes placed on the megaphone portion, while another person pushes it along by the handlebars in the back. See close-ups of it, as well as other photos of the Enchanted Forest, at **craftzine.com/04/forest**.

FOUND WEARABLES: As leader of Austin's Art Ninjas, artninjas.com, **Joey Sue Roberts** works with found objects, turning them into jewelry.

RECLAIMED METAL ART: A traditionally trained blacksmith from Baltimore, **Megan "Molly" Whitten** recently started making jewelry because it was more mobile. She and Albert are the resident pack rats. She's constantly saving and collecting found metal and objects for the other artists to use.

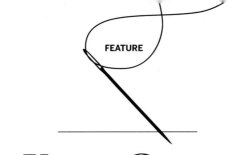

Not Your Grandpa's
EMBROIDERY

BY ANNA DILEMNA

Modern men enjoy a craft that wasn't always thought of as "women's work."

These days if you want to do some showing off, you can just cover yourself from head to toe in Burberry plaid and call it a day. A few hundred years ago, people did things a bit differently.

Say the local feudal lord was dropping by for tea and you wanted to make sure he was duly impressed. First you might have some decorative stitching done on that cunning little cap you just bought. And what about those drab draperies in the grand chamber? Better have those embroidered as well.

But who did you call for the job? Grandma? Not likely. Up until the mid-19th century, it was primarily men who were in high demand as professional embroiderers for folks who wanted to show a bit of bling. More likely you'd have commissioned Great-Great-Great-Great-Grandpa!

During the Industrial Revolution, machines were invented that made it easy to embroider on a massive scale. The demand for individual artisans dropped, and with it the prestige associated with owning fine embroidered goods. In short order, the practice became relegated to the realm of "women's work," its long association with men all but forgotten. These days you can imagine Grandma stitching away while watching Lawrence Welk, or maybe you know some hipster girl who just finished an embroidered portrait of Peaches. But a hipster guy with a needle and embroidery floss?

Luckily, there are some men who are willing to defy modern gender stereotypes by continuing in the steps of their stitchy forefathers. Matthew Cox emphasizes the connection between stitching and healing by embroidering directly onto medical X-rays. His portraits add humanity and even humor to items that are generally associated with unfeeling sterility. A small white skull sports a mass of yellow Shirley Temple ringlets; a bare femur bone pokes out of a field of wildflowers. The unique combinations humanize not only the X-rays, but the stitched images as well. How did the owner of this ankle with the embroidered tennis shoe get hurt? A trampoline trick gone wrong, or just a routine jogging injury?

Another fan of unorthodox canvases is Steve MacDonald, who has embroidered on everything from skateboard decks to cuckoo clocks. With an

> *Up until the mid-19th century, it was primarily men who were in high demand as professional embroiderers.*

old Singer sewing machine, Steve stitches mad mélanges of tigers, deer, bike tracks, and sprawling cityscapes. The resulting work looks futuristic, and at the same time brings to mind the magical style of an antique Japanese ukiyo-e print.

MacDonald and Cox are quite literally holding onto the threads of history, albeit with some very modern twists of their own that make it clear: this is not your grandpa's embroidery. ✂

Steve MacDonald: ramblinworker.com
Matthew Cox: jonathanferraragallery.com, packergallery.com, and finerthingsgallery.com

Anna Dilemna is a doll maker and writer. See her work at annadilemna.typepad.com.

Photography by: Bill Cramer (top left), Jen Siska (top right), Steve MacDonald (middle and bottom right), Matthew Cox (bottom left)

CLOCKWISE FROM TOP LEFT:
Matthew Cox reaches out with Ribcage;
Steve MacDonald in his studio; MacDonald's
surreal landscapes, Tiger Over Cityscape *and*
Smokestack; *an anonymous foot gets a new*
sneaker in Ankle, *by Cox.*

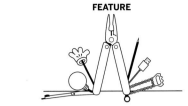

What the Hell
IS THAT THING?

BY GARETH BRANWYN

The world of weird and wonderful crafting tools.

Every area of human activity seems to boast its own toolset. This is certainly the case in arts and crafts, where nearly every step in a process can have its own tool. Need to glue something? There are tools to prepare the surface, apply the glue, hold the pieces together, and clean up the components afterward. While this tool profusion can get gluttonous, some of the strangest and most frivolous-seeming tools can prove the most useful. Here's a rundown of wacky-looking devices we think you'll appreciate in your tool chest.

» Helping Hands

DIY

In electronics, a helping hand, or third hand, is a device for holding circuit boards or other parts for soldering. You can buy them at places like RadioShack, but building your own is really easy, and you can design yours with as many "hands" as you like (commercial models usually have only two).

All you need is a piece of scrap wood as your base, some heavy-gauge copper wire, and alligator clips attached to the ends of the wire. Staple as many of these two-handed "arms" as you want. You can use your homemade helping hands for holding project pieces to solder, glue, paint, sandblast, etc.

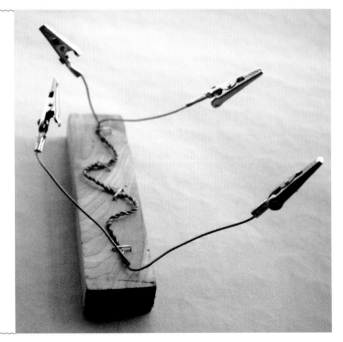

Photography by Sam Murphy

Gareth Branwyn is a regular contributor to MAKE (makezine.com) and writes widely about do-it-yourself technologies. He also runs the personal tech website Street Tech (streettech.com).

« Crop-A-Dile

We R Memory Keepers $27

If ever a tool deserved the proverbial WTF!?, it's this thingamajig. Like a hole punch on steroids, the Crop-a-Dile has two heavy-duty punchers that can burrow into material as gnarly as chipboard, and as hard as metal. It installs snaps, eyelets, and decorative buttons, and comes in eight different colors.

» Foam Cutter

Wonder Cutter $13

Insulation foam makes a reasonably dense, strong, yet lightweight material for sculpting, modeling, and decorating. But it can be hard and messy to cut, especially if you want curves. Foam Cutter to the rescue! This inexpensive gadget holds a hot wire that'll cut through foam like buttah.

« Rotary Paper Edger

Fiskars $8

Working on a desktop-produced CD, the art designer told me to get a "perfing tool" for folding the covers and tray cards. So I found this widget, the Fiskars Paper Edger. It has a 45mm toothed wheel that perfs as you roll. Perfect for neat folding, especially on thick stock, and to create tear-off sections.

» Pin Vise

Zona Tool $7

A pin vise is a holder of small-diameter drill bits that allows you to manually twist holes into wood, plastic, soft metals, and more. When I first saw one, I couldn't imagine it was effective, but The Zona, especially, with its large wooden handle, allows you to apply plenty of torque.

« Ultra ShapeXpress

Fiskars $18

It may look like some kid's science toy, but the ShapeXpress is a devilishly sharp cutter that can be used with stencils and plastic templates to cut out various shapes in paper or other thin materials, or you can use it freehand. Either way, it's much easier than using a hobby knife or swivel-blade cutter. ✕

Business Basics
FOR CRAFTY TYPES

BY JENNY RYAN

The essentials for transforming your craft from hobby to business.

Ready to make the leap from crafting as a hobby to crafting as a vocation? The transition can be a bumpy one, especially if you haven't done your homework. As a crafty business owner, you'll have to grow comfortable wearing many different hats, not just making them.

Designing and creating your products is just one facet of the job — you'll also be responsible for accounting, marketing, shipping, customer service, and more. Time management is also an issue, as you'll need to be prepared to put in far more hours than you'd work at a day job. However, as entrepreneur Susie Ghahremani (boygirlparty.com) notes, "Every day I enjoy my business and feel satisfied, and I can't say I ever had a 'real' job that made me feel so proud of my work and personal growth."

Before handing your walking papers to The Man, take time to educate yourself. Many community colleges offer classes in small business management, web design, and bookkeeping. Full-time crafter Tess Lee (madebytess.com) took a few classes in Dreamweaver and Photoshop, and highly recommends the experience for anyone interested in working for herself. "Even if you don't design your own website, you can do your own updates," Lee explains. "I'm a big DIY-er and want to do everything with my own two hands, if at all possible."

The vast majority of crafters operate their businesses as **sole proprietors**, which means using your Social Security number to register your business. Call your State Board of Equalization (BOE), and follow their instructions on how to obtain a **resale license**, which allows you to legally sell your goods. You'll be required to collect and file taxes on these sales, so be sure to factor this into your prices. Having a resale license also means you can purchase craft supplies at wholesale prices, which is a must if you hope to make a profit selling your wares. Some states allow you to file your license via mail, but visiting your BOE in person can be a valuable experience, especially if you have questions — they are often free and easy with business advice and useful reading materials for new business owners. Overall, filing for your resale license is a simple (and usually free) process.

If you plan on using a business name other than your own, you should also file a **fictitious name statement** (also called a **DBA** for "doing business as"); this too is as simple as filling out a form, usually at your County Recorder's office. Once your paperwork is filed, you're usually required to publish a notice in a local newspaper announcing your DBA. When you get your DBA paperwork back, it will be accompanied by offers from various newspapers to run your DBA notice. Choose the best deal, and you'll probably end up spending less than $75 altogether.

Once your DBA is in place, you'll be able to open a bank account under your business name, which comes in handy if you want to be able to cash checks made out to "Kuddlekrafts," or whatever your business name might be.

Depending on where you live, you may also need a city **business license** and/or **home occupation permit** — contact your city's Office of Finance to make sure. The filing fee (if any) will vary from city to city, and many cities offer small-business exemptions, meaning you won't pay any city business taxes if you make under a certain amount

each year (in Los Angeles, for instance, the amount is $100,000). If a license or permit is required, be sure to renew it annually; otherwise you risk being fined.

With the help of accounting software like QuickBooks, most business owners can handle filing their **sales and use taxes** on their own (the BOE will send you the tax forms automatically once you have your resale license). When filing your **federal income taxes**, though, it's wise to seek professional help.

"File often and early!" recommends Kellee Milner (myfavoritemirror.com). "Find someone who is knowledgeable with your particular business structure right from the get-go. The ins and outs they know can bring you huge peace of mind. I'd rather pay someone to handle that kind of thing for me so that I know it's being done right, and that nothing is being left out, than to have all that stress come April trying to figure it all out on my own."

So now that you're legal, where do you sell your stuff? It's easier than ever to set up an **online shop**, and sites like etsy.com, shopify.com, and mintd.com are quick, simple, and affordable options for creating a virtual storefront — especially for crafters with limited web skills.

If you'd rather run your own website, there are several designers specializing in creating smaller, craft-oriented sites: lightningbugdesigns.com, redlimeweb.com, and smartandlovely.com are just a few.

The importance of having an internet presence can't be overstated. "I actually started my current crafty business about six months before I had a web-site," shares Cathy Callahan (cathyofcalifornia.com). "Things just *exploded* the second I launched my site."

Having a website is no good unless people find out about it, of course. "Keeping a blog, or sending out some sort of update email is very important," says with four years experience under her belt. "Swapping links with other small businesses is great, too."

Networking can help in a myriad of ways — a friend may be willing to swap a business card design for one of your homemade bath scrubs, for instance. Any way you can get the word out and grow your business while keeping costs low is worth looking into. **Vending at craft fairs** will increase your sales and your visibility, so keep plenty of postcards, buttons, or other promotional items on hand. You may pick up some wholesale accounts this way as well.

However far you decide to go with your crafty business, it takes effort to stay the course. Remember that your aim is to earn a living, and if you price your items too low you'll end up barely breaking even, a sure recipe for business burnout. Be realistic about your goals and step outside the craft room from time to time. As Nicole Vasbinder (queenpuffpuff.com) advises, "Working from home can be lonely, and the days can run together. Keep your spirit and mind fresh, and your work will continue to be inspired." ✂

➕ More resources at craftzine.com/04/business

Jenny Ryan is a crafter living in Los Angeles with her cartoonist husband, Johnny, and their two insane cats. She is owner of sewdarncute.com and the organizer of Felt Club (feltclub.com), L.A.'s popular indie craft fair.

Illustration by Kate O'Leary

Joss Paper Stacking Trays

A mess of stuff on a tabletop never looks like a mess of stuff on a tabletop if it's contained in an artful tray. Some cheap building materials and a quick trip to Chinatown (or Asian Superstore kkdiscount.com) are all you need to do a little mess management with some tabletop exotica.

You will need: Luan board (thin plywood), miter box, 1⅛" outside corner Clearwood trim, sandpaper, newspaper, spray paint, spray adhesive, joss paper (thin decorative paper sold in Chinese import shops), plain copy or printer paper, wood glue, mixing container, stirring stick, EnviroTex Pour-On Gloss Finish

1. Size and cut.

Cut the luan board to the desired tray sizes (pictured trays measure 14"×18", 10"×14", and 7"×10"), then miter-cut the corner trim to fit each tray bottom. Sand the edges of the corner trim and the tray bottoms.

2. Spray.

Spray corner trim pieces with 2 coats of metallic paint. Over newspaper, spray adhesive on the backsides of the joss paper and position them onto the top (dark side) of the luan board, as you like. Lay a sheet of printer paper over the joss to square and smooth the joss by hand. Fold excess joss over the edge of the luan board and press flat. Cover each board.

3. Glue.

Square the trim onto a newspaper-covered tabletop, and run a line of wood glue on the bottom inside edge. Place the tray bottom joss-side-up inside the corner trim frame, and let dry.

4. Pour.

Mix gloss finish as per product instructions. Generously pour finish into each tray, covering completely. Once the finish has coated the entire surface, place the tray on a level, newspaper-covered tabletop to dry.

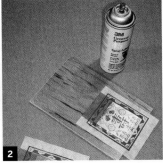

Matt Maranian is a best-selling writer, designer, and bon vivant whose books include *PAD* and *PAD Parties*. He lives in New England.

Photography by Matt Maranian

FANCY DRESS

Photograph by Robyn Twomey

YO HO, YO HO, A PIRATE PUG'S COSTUME FOR ME!

COSTUMES THROUGH THE AGES

From devilish beasts to Daniel Boone.
BY JOY EMERY

DARK AGES

Medieval pageants were all the rage, where devils, saints, and religious figures were impersonated.

1600s

Elaborate Italian carnivals influenced all of Europe. Venetian revelers of all classes donned fanciful costumes and masks, or voluminous cloaks called dominos.

1700s

Fancy balls flourished in England, where costumes and masks concealed wearers' identities. The anonymity provided opportunity for a wide range of society to participate, and led to inevitable intrigue and decadence. Popular characters included commedia dell'arte characters such as Harlequin, Columbine, and Pantaloon, as well as exotic fashions of the Orient, Africa, and North America. Low-life characters such as chimney sweeps and milkmaids were also represented.

Joy Spanabel Emery, curator of the Commercial Pattern Archive at the University of Rhode Island, is professor emeritus of theatre and was the resident costume designer. She is the author of *Stage Costume Techniques* and numerous articles on the history of dressmaker patterns.

Illustrations by Melinda Beck

Fancy dress – or costuming –

has been a part of Western culture throughout history because people of all ages love to dress up and pretend. For children and adults, pretending to be someone or something else lets you into a fantasy world, like being Cinderella at the ball. Inhibitions can be put aside for a bit when one is disguised — it can be magical.

1800s

Emphasis shifted from anonymity to inventiveness and conspicuous display. Allegorical figures such as Night, Spring, or Rose Garden mingled with butterflies and hornets. Fascination with medieval chivalry also dominated, like kings, queens, and knights, as well as folk heroes such as Robin Hood. Queen Victoria and Prince Albert gave many fancy dress balls, often themed to a particular historical period.

Wealthy society in the States held lavish balls. Couturiers were commissioned to design and make richly embellished costumes. Other, less expensive sources included costume rental houses and paper patterns for homemade costumes. Sensing a lucrative market, companies produced catalogs devoted to a range of costume possibilities.

1900s

World War I severely diminished the popularity of wearing fancy dress. However, in the euphoria after the war there was a resurgence, and once again costumes were disguises complete with masks.

The shift in society's use of leisure time after World War II, with TV and backyard barbecues, along with an increasing interest in reenacting historical times such as the American Civil War, supplanted fancy dress balls. However, the desire to experience the magic of dressing up and disguising oneself did not totally disappear. When October 31st rolls around, we'll see countless princesses, Hogwarts characters, and film creatures that carry on the tradition of dressing up that goes back to the Romans. It's trick-or-treat rather than fancy dress balls.

Heavenly Hoopla

Annie Weinert designs costumes that shimmer and flow.

BY VICTORIA EVERMAN

Halloween is the first thought that comes to most minds when you mention costumes: vampires and superheroes, ghosts and princesses. Living in a fantasy world for one day a year is a treat for the multitude. But not for one 25-year-old: "I've always loved costumes for the sheer joy of getting decked out and parading around; costuming once a year wasn't enough for me!"

Annie Weinert (annieland.net) has moved beyond the ghouls and goblins of that infamous October night (though last year she went as fantastic candy corn). Since she began working with the HoopGirl AllStars (hoopgirl.com), a San Francisco hula-hoop performance troupe, costume renditions of Bettie Page and neon cyber-geishas have become the norm.

Weinert's leap from weekend hooper to professional started one innocent day in the park. "Christabel [Zamor, founder of HoopGirl] was walking by and approached me when she saw the hoops, and we connected." Fast-forward two years, and Weinert is now making the stage costumes for the six-girl attraction and performing with them as well. In addition, solo performances at Ruby Skye, one of San Francisco's biggest nightclubs, have given her an unprecedented opportunity to showcase her most unique creations.

Unlike traditional movie or theater costuming, designing costumes for hooping has its own challenges. "Color, texture, movement, and functionality all inform my designs," Weinert explains. "For instance, I noticed that having long fringe and flowing materials on the legs looks amazing while turning and jumping."

Vinyl, stretchy metallic lamés, faux fur, and garters are just a few of her favorite features — the more colorful and flamboyant, the better. Part of being onstage is getting noticed, and you'll have no problem fixing your eyes on the girls with the twirling, clear PVC, flashing LED, light-up hula hoops.

The impeccably positive, joyous energy that Weinert exudes is a quaint parallel to her designs. "Sewing [is] a way to remind myself to not take life too seriously. It is a wonderful creative outlet for my silliness."

Dancing in front of a few hundred people while dressed as a space cyborg would qualify as pretty darn silly, but it's also great exercise. After learning about HoopGirl, Weinert attended one of the growing number of hooping classes they hold in the Bay Area. Today, she's a certified hoopdance instructor.

Expanding beyond hooping costumes is the next step for Weinert's new business, Annieland. Having sold her costumes at music festivals, she knows people love them. "I figure there's nothing wrong with thinking big! I would love to be able to travel all over the world performing and selling my costumes."

Whether working for a large group or a unique individual, custom attention is the core of her creative endeavor. "I like to take personalities into consideration when I'm choosing colors and patterns. I want my customers to feel like their costume is an expression of their unique style as well as mine."

With four years of costuming experience under her belt, and many more to come, it's crystal clear that Weinert has a crafty future ahead. "I put a lot of time and energy into what I do, but it doesn't feel like hard work because I adore it. Each [costume is a] representation of where I was in life. They capture step by step my changing flow of creative energy." ✕

Victoria Everman is a writer, model, and environmentalist in San Francisco. Her many creative endeavors, including founding the SF Craft Mafia, can be found at victoria-e.com.

Photograph by Gabriela Hasbun at the Red Poppy Art House, San Francisco (redpoppyarthouse.org); paintings: *Fugitives 2000/2001* by Rafael Landea

HOOP ACTION: Annie Weinert sends audiences into orbit with her stellar HoopGirl costumes.

Burlesque Bouquet

Pile on the fruit for a Carmen Miranda-style headdress.

BY ANGIE PONTANI

I've always had an affinity for over-the-top embellishments — gold fleck paint on a mirror, glitter-encrusted twigs in an oversized floral arrangement. I think my Italian-American, East Coast heritage has something to do with this affliction of mine.

For years, I didn't know where to direct my desire to bedazzle everything in sight, until one Halloween when my creative parents dressed me as the grape cluster from a Fruit of the Loom commercial. Completing the spectacle of foam balls spray-painted green and sewn to a unitard was a headdress made from a glittering twisted twig, adorned with a rhinestone-embellished grape leaf. My parents strapped it to my head, and my life officially began.

I became a headdress maniac, and as all headdress maniacs must do, I became obsessed with the mother of us all, Carmen Miranda. Best known for her fruit-basket head arrangements, she literally rocked hundreds of towering cornucopias filled with everything from fruit to butterflies to silk ribbons and glittering stars. If it could be dreamed, it could be worn, and this concept moved me to no end.

When I started my burlesque troupe, the World Famous Pontani Sisters, in 1999, it was a no-brainer that one of our first acts would be a mambo — a tribute to Carmen and to my Italian heritage. Hence, Mambo Italiano was born. For this I created three towering fruit headdresses, covered in rhinestones, silk flowers, and glittering baskets, measuring 1½ feet high. The act has toured a dozen times, performing everywhere from New York to Los Angeles.

I find headdresses the ultimate expression in costuming. Whether it's feathers, baskets, or simple hair combs, they allow you to turn a fabulous costume into a truly sensational creation. »

Materials

» **STRAW BASKET** FOR THIS BEGINNER MODEL, I PREFER A PLATE-LIKE BASKET WITH LOW SIDES, WITH AN APPROXIMATELY 9" DIAMETER.

» **SPANDEX BLEND FABRIC (1 YARD)** THIS IS USED TO TIE THE BASKET TO YOUR HEAD, AND ITS STRETCH ENABLES YOU TO FEEL SECURE. AFTER YOU BECOME MORE COMFORTABLE, YOU CAN USE ALMOST ANY TYPE OF FABRIC. I PREFER SILK CREPE.

» **STYROFOAM HEAD** FOUND AT WIG AND WELL-STOCKED BEAUTY SUPPLY SHOPS

» **T-PINS OR EXTRA-LONG STRAIGHT PINS**

» **ASSORTED PLASTIC FRUIT (12 PIECES)** OFTEN FOUND AT CRAFT STORES AND FLORAL SHOPS

» **ASSORTED FAKE FLOWERS WITH LEAVES (6–12)**

» **FELT (1 YARD)** ANY COLOR, SINCE IT WON'T SHOW

» **GLUE GUN AND HOT MELT GLUE STICKS**

» **X-ACTO KNIFE**

» **IRON**

» **NEEDLE AND THREAD TO MATCH FABRIC**

Photograph by Beth Perkins

SITTING PRETTY: Angie Pontani wears her daily serving of fresh fruit.

FANCY DRESS

START »

1. SEW THE HEADDRESS TIE.
Cut your fabric 12" wide and 50" long. Fold in half lengthwise, then sew the open edges together with a strong, tight stitch (by hand or machine). You will have something that resembles a 6"-wide belt with openings at both ends (like a flat fabric tube). Stitch one of the open ends with a tight stitch.

Invert your material (turn it inside out, which is actually right side in), and turn in the one remaining open side, as if you were doing a hem. Secure with straight pins, and stitch closed. Warm iron flat.

2. MAKE TIE SLITS AND THREAD HEAD TIE.
Using your X-Acto knife, make two 3" slices in your basket, one on either side of where it will sit on your head, at least 2" in from the outer edges, and at least 3" away from each other. Thread your fabric through your new slits. Start underneath your basket, pull up through the top, lay it flat across the center, then pull down through the other side.

3. HOT-GLUE THE FABRIC.
With your hot glue gun, seal the openings to the fabric, and seal the fabric to the basket. Don't worry if the glue drips through the openings — just make sure it doesn't burn your fingers!

Remember — like hair mousse and rouge, less is more when it comes to hot glue guns. A small amount will give you a fabulous bond and look much neater.

4. LINE THE BASKET WITH FELT.
Lining the basket helps secure the head tie and also makes the fruit bond better. Cut your felt to the size of the interior diameter of your basket, then apply hot glue to the felt before laying it in the basket.

Mount your headdress on a styrofoam head until it cools. You can use T-pins or extra long straight pins to secure it.

5. ADD THE FRUIT AND GARNISH.
Experiment with layering your fruit in the basket. I prefer bananas down low and in front, but it's a personal choice. When you have the first layer in an order you like, note where the fruit touches the basket. Hot glue clean lines onto the fruit before placing them on the basket. Hold them firmly in place until the glue dries. Then build upon the bottom layer of fruit by gluing more fruit on top of it. Use the flowers and leaves to fill in any open spots. Allow the headdress to cool, feel for any loose fruits or flowers, and secure with more hot glue. ✂

Angie Pontani is the founding member of the World Famous Pontani Sisters (pontanisisters.com). She lives in Brooklyn, N.Y., with her ferociously adorable dog, Elvis-Louise.

Photography by Sam Murphy

Photograph by Beth Perkins

> ❝ Carmen Miranda literally rocked hundreds of towering cornucopias filled with everything from fruit to butterflies to silk ribbons and glittering stars. ❞

COSPLAY

Anime fans transform into their favorite characters.

BY ANNE McKNIGHT

Each summer, in the dry, shimmering heat of Southern California, 40,000 people gather for the country's largest anime convention, Anime Expo. Two-thirds of the attendees will not be sporting the sensible shoes and free swag bags typical of conventioneers. They will be dressed in cosplay regalia: carefully tailored, mostly handmade costumes, helmets, and tiaras based on anime cartoons, manga comic books, or video game characters.

You can catch them on their way to compete in the convention's centerpiece, the masquerade competition, or simply to testify to their fandom by strutting their stuff in the suites and sidewalks of the convention center.

Cosplay, a term that combines the words *costume* and *play*, is a thriving subculture with unique Japan-Los Angeles roots. In the late 70s and early 80s, sci-fi fans exchanged videos and anime by day, and partied by night, often dressing up as their favorite characters. These parties came to be called "masquerades." Japanese critics familiar with the California scene popularized the masquerade at events like Comiket, the huge DIY zine and comic market held twice a year in Tokyo.

But cosplay differs between Japan and North America. In Japan, people dress up for special events like Comiket. But the masquerade — a competition showcasing the artful making of costumes — is a North American invention. The cosplay masquerade has its roots in two traditions: 1) the aristocratic masked ball, familiar to cosplayers from *The Rose of Versailles*, the phenomenally popular girls' manga that emerged in the 70s; and 2) the talent contest. During a masquerade, a cosplay team will compete for two prizes — craftsmanship and presentation — by performing a choreographed routine to a prerecorded song or skit, which is often a parody of or homage to a known anime scene.

"Around 2002, the bar really rose for [cosplay] costume design," says Mandy Mitchell, who's been involved in cosplay since 1999. No longer could people sport store-bought costumes, or disposable Halloween swords. People began learning how to sew, and to scavenge garment districts and hardware stores for unusual fabrics, patterns, and industrial materials. These days, Mitchell explains, by venturing into unexplored areas of pattern catalogs — such as figure skating designs to adapt for the *Sailor Moon* bodice — "you can find a pattern for almost anything you want to make."

The team of "magical" girls in *Sailor Moon* is a popular choice for costumes. The most beloved anime since the 90s, *Sailor Moon* features a team of ordinary girls who morph out of their everyday lives to take on the identities of heroic fighters. As each schoolgirl in the anime actualizes her identity as a soldier of love and justice, her uniform transforms into a dazzling version of its everyday self.

Lynleigh Benton, a costumer with a background in fashion design, notes that because of the variety of characters and its popularity, "everybody does a Sailor Senshi [warrior] once in their life."

For a cosplayer, the magical transformation into a sexy warrior takes place through the detailed design and crafting of costumes, highlighting the independence and creativity that define each character. Benton's Sailor Uranus costume features a satin skirt, fitted spandex bodice, and platform boots. It took 100 hours to make, and demanded that she draft special patterns for the sleeves and bow, as well as make a skirt of flounces that look pleated, almost two-dimensional. For some, this may seem tedious, but not when anime is your passion. To participate in cosplay, says Benton, who makes, on average, ten costumes a year, "first and foremost, you have to be a fan" of the character you are cosplaying. ✄

Anne McKnight writes and teaches about Japanese literature and subculture at USC in Los Angeles.

Photography by: Yas Satô (2 and 7), and Kyle Johnson of cosplay.com (4 and 6). Illustrations by: Ikeda Riyoko (1) from *Rose of Versailles All Color Illustration Book*, and Takeichi Naoko (3 and 5) from *Bishoujo Senshi Sailor Moon Original Picture Collections Volumes 4 and 5*.

By venturing into unexplored areas of pattern catalogs — such as figure skating designs to adapt for the *Sailor Moon* bodice — you can find a pattern for almost anything you want to make.

1 2 Marie Antoinette, from Ikeda Riyoko's phenomenally popular *Rose of Versailles* manga. The first design is taken from the manga art book. The second is Lynleigh Benton's adaptation, based on a Renaissance-style dress, drawing on some design elements from other parts of the manga.

5 6 Eternal Sailor Uranus is one of the guardians of the Sailor Moon character, charged with controlling the air and skies. Her tomboyish look, a magical version of a schoolgirl uniform, features a satin skirt, satin spandex bodice, platform boots, and choker necklace.

3 A sketch for the *Sailor Moon* anime program, with Sailor Moon flanked by her guardian warriors.
4 The Eternal Sailor troupe, soldiers of love and justice, at Anime Expo 2006 in Anaheim, Calif. First from the left is Lynleigh Benton (Sailor Uranus), and third from the right is Mandy Mitchell (Sailor Mars).

7 An elegant Gothic Lolita ensemble. Goth-Loli is a fashion style, rather than a costume: it's not attached to any particular story or character. It emphasizes an elegant sensibility and black-and-white design, and is often composed of motifs like strawberries, flounces, lace, and parasols.

CALLING ALL SALTY SEA DOGS

Your matey will look shipshape in this piratical costume.

BY ANDREA DeHART

I've never owned a store-bought costume. I was one of those kids lucky enough to have a super crafty mom who would jump on her sewing machine and whip up anything from a placemat to a prom dress without hesitation. When Halloween came around each year, she would fulfill our wildest fantasies no matter what the request. I loved my homemade costumes, and no other kid in school had a custom costume like mine. Following in my mom's footsteps, I too enjoy the thrill of the challenge. So when I was asked to design a canine costume, I said, "Aye, Cap'n!"

If you're looking to turn your dog pal into a swashbuckling seafarer with style, set your sights on this project. Moderate sewing skills are required, but the supplies will only set you back a couple of doubloons. Although the outfit was created for a pug, you can easily alter the pattern pieces to fit most small dogs.

Pirate accoutrements complete the costume; included in the pattern are a functional pirate hat and belt. Don't forget to pick up a miniature fake parrot for the shoulder (or train yours if you have a real one). Other pirate pizzazz to plunder: a small toy sword, a pouch filled with gold coins, an eye patch, a treasure chest, a large bone, and some gold hoop earrings.

Mass-market costumes can walk the plank! »

Andrea DeHart, aka CraftyBitch (**craftybitch.com**) **is the creator of handmade handbags, wallets, doggie couture, and most recently, a little girl.**

MATERIALS

ADD EXTRA YARDAGE FOR A LARGER DOG.

» ½YD 60"-WIDE, RED AND WHITE STRIPED, STRETCH KNIT FABRIC (FOR SHIRT)

» ¼YD 45"-WIDE, RED, RIB KNIT FABRIC

» ½YD 45"-WIDE, MEDIUM-WEIGHT, BLACK SATIN FABRIC (FOR PANTS)

» 6" LENGTH OF ¾" RED HOOK-AND-LOOP FASTENER TAPE

» 10" LENGTH OF ¾" BLACK HOOK-AND-LOOP FASTENER TAPE

» 3" GOLD BUTTONS (2)

» 9"x12" PIECE OF 2MM WHITE FOAM SHEET OR PRE-CUT, WHITE, ADHESIVE FOAM SKULL AND CROSSBONES, PATCH OR STICKER, 2" OR SMALLER

» 12"x18" PIECE OF 3MM BLACK FOAM SHEET

» ⅔YD 6" FLAT GOLD BRAID TRIM

» 1YD ¼" CLEAR ELASTIC

» SMALL FAKE PARROT

» CRAFT GLUE, HOLE PUNCH, COMMON SEWING SUPPLIES

» PATTERNS FROM CRAFTZINE.COM/04/PIRATE

FIT FOR A DOG: Bella the scurvy pirate pug drools over her ill-gotten booty while adrift at sea.

Photograph by Robyn Twomey

FANCY DRESS

START »

GENERAL ASSEMBLY GUIDELINES: All seam allowances are ¼" unless otherwise noted. See pattern pieces for notes on making size adjustments.

1. CUT OUT AND SEW THE SHIRT
1a. To begin, cut all the fabric pieces out, using the patterns at craftzine.com/04/pirate.

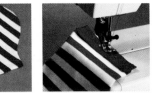

1b. Fold the cuffs lengthwise with the wrong sides together, and pin to the right side of the sleeves. Slightly stretch cuffs to match the notches on the sleeves, and sew. Repeat for neckband.

1c. Press the seam allowances toward the body.

1d. Attach the sleeves to the bodice, matching notches around the armholes.

1e. Sew the sleeves closed beginning at the cuff, along the underarm, and continuing across the front chest. Finish the bottom edge of the shirt by pressing under ¼" and topstitching.

1f. On the right center chest seam, turn under 1" and baste closed. Pin the appropriate length of loop tape fastener on the side of the shirt that faces inward. Sew around all 4 sides of fastener. On the left side of the center chest seam, sew the matching length of hook tape on the side of the shirt that faces outward.

1g. Attach the parrot to the shoulder by using a whipstitch around the bird's legs. (Some come with a wire extending from the legs that can also be used to secure the bird to the shirt.)

2. SEW THE PANTS
2a. Run a basting stitch ⅛" and another ½" from the bottom of the leg opening between the notches.

2b. Pull the basting stitches to gather the pants, matching notches on the band. With the right sides together, pin and sew the 2 pieces together. Remove the basting stitches.

2c. Turn under ¼" on the raw edge of the band pieces, and press. Fold band lengthwise and baste in place. On the outside of the pants, topstitch the top of the band.

Photography by Andrea DeHart

2d. Finish the bottom edge of the pants and back opening by pressing under ¼" and topstitching.

2e. Turn under 1" on the rear side of the pant leg inner seam and baste closed. Pin the appropriate length of loop tape fastener to the inside of this fold. Sew around all 4 sides of the fastener. On the opposite side of the pant leg inner seam, sew the matching length of hook tape to the front.

2f. Sew a gold button on the outer side of each pant leg band, centered. With right sides together, sew the shirt to the pants at the waist with a ½" seam allowance. Press the seams open.

3. **MAKE THE HAT**
3a. From the pattern, cut hat shape from the 3mm black foam sheet, then center the skull detail and secure with craft glue.

3b. Close the hat by overlapping the side flaps in the back, and glue. Next, glue the gold trim close to the edge at the top of the hat.

3c. Punch 4 holes at the bottom of the hat, matching the dots on the pattern. Thread clear elastic through the holes as shown, to create the Y-shaped strap. Secure the open end of the elastic to the strap, 3" from the bottom of the hat, by folding under ½" and hand-stitching with thread in an X formation.

4. **MAKE THE BELT**
4a. Glue gold trim around the edge of the buckle. Center the skull detail and secure with glue.

4b. Measure the dog's waist, around the seam where the shirt and pants meet, and add 4". You may need to cut 2 strips of the 3mm foam sheet to get the desired length (they can meet underneath the middle of the buckle). Once cut, center the buckle in the middle of the belt, and glue.

4c. Cut two 2" strips of loop tape and position them horizontally on the top side of one end of the belt. Cut two 2" strips of hook tape and position them vertically on the bottom side of the opposite end of the belt. Glue all pieces in place. ✕

ADD ALTERNATE ACCESSORIES:
Feel free to add extra props to the belt, such as a dangling pouch of gold coins or a small toy sword. Also consider a feather, pirate flag, treasure chest, eye patch, bandana, hook, or wooden leg.

🔲 See our princess pooch costume at craftzine.com/04/princess.

Final photograph by Robyn Twomey

SPiRit GiRl

Marnie Weber's ghostly clowns and dancing animals venture to the otherworld.

BY ANNIE BUCKLEY

Marnie Weber's fascinating world of singing flowers, masked mermaids, wise bears, and ghostly clowns walks a fine line between dream and reality. Weber has made a career of weaving together diverse media through the use of surreal narrative, and if each story line is the conceptual glue, costumes are the physical mainstay. A spectacular array of costumes winds through Weber's multi-media work, appearing in her films, sculptures, videos, collages, performances, and installations.

A former member of the Los Angeles band Party Boys, Weber incorporates music and performance into her art. Since her earliest performance, *Of Marnie, Of Rat, Of Caryatids* at Rebel Art Gallery in Hollywood (1987), costumes have been central. She recalls, "I only did one performance not in character, and it was such an uncomfortable experience that I thought, 'I better go in character,' and it really freed me up." Freed her up, indeed. In the 20 years since, Weber has developed a highly original and complex body of work where costumes continue to play a vital role, from gallery to theater to screen.

Weber uses thrift store castoffs and basic craft materials like fabric and fur, glitter and glue, and papier-mâché, but the key ingredients are her vivid imagination, sensitivity to character, and eye for possibility. A basketball piñata, child's animal mask, and jar of modeling paste are put together to become a bear, possum, or bunny. On seeing foam trophy heads in a taxidermy catalog, she thought, "It would be so great to wear those on top of a helmet!" and she figured out how to do it. The resulting totem-like headgear, worn by characters in her 2007 film, *A Western Song*, encapsulates

Weber's striking combination of realism and fantasy.

One of the most evocative things about the costumes is how they so effectively transform their wearers, including Weber, who dons them in her live performances, videos, and films. She refers to them not as costumes but as characters. "It's hard for me to think of them as nonliving things," she explains. "Even when they're on a mannequin, they seem to carry a spirit with them, and you get a feeling for the personality, even if it's not moving."

The wizened face of the possum is a perfect example, a recurring favorite since its first appearance in her 2001 video, *The Forgotten*. Its head is made from the combination of two masks — a giraffe and an old woman. More recently, the Dandy Clowns, which began as masks "picked up in a costume shop," are transformed into expressive faces that feel more like people than masks.

Though they have evolved over the years, from simple to more complex, each character retains a dreamlike sense of fantasy moored in reality, a hallmark of Weber's work. Earlier characters were made primarily from thrift store finds. For *Coquette Circus Girl* (1993), Weber wore a drum majorette top and a skirt tinged with Christmas tree tinsel. She carried a child's blue guitar and impaled herself through a large stuffed pony. As her work progressed, Weber began to make more elaborate costumes, expanding her ingenuity more than her shopping list. In her studio, she is constantly playing, piecing together new combinations, seeing what works, and unearthing a style of crafting as straightforward as her work is otherworldly.

Costuming and crafting came early to Weber,

Photograph by Robert Yeager

Even when they're on a mannequin, they seem to carry a spirit with them, and you get a feeling for the personality.

PREVIOUS PAGE: Weber and the Dandy Clowns CLOCKWISE FROM TOP LEFT: *Coquette Circus Girl*, 1993; *A Western Song*, production still, 2007; *Songs That Never Die*, production still, 2005; *The Bunny*, 2001.

who retains fond memories of making elaborate Halloween costumes as a child with her father. "All girls [dress up], but I think the difference was that I had my dad helping me with my costumes from an early age, and it's just one of the things that we did together. He used to put a lot of work into my costumes, and I think that was the inspiring part — that I saw them from scratch to finish. I thought, 'Oh, I could do this myself probably, eventually.' And so I did."

She recalls winning an award for a bush costume (attaching branches to a green leotard) that sounds like a precursor to the flower-women in her 2005 rock opera, *Songs That Never Die*, in which enormous petals, made from fabric dipped in glue, frame the faces of women wrapped in gauze.

The bush costume may have won a prize, but it's the love of invention and make-believe that's had a lasting influence. Even as Weber rises in status in an international art world that often favors slick over homemade, technology over craft, it's important to her that the work maintains a DIY sensibility.

"I want to inspire people," she explains. "And I don't feel like you can inspire people if the work is so extremely technically crafted and professional that it would make people just feel like, 'I should never bother doing anything like that 'cause I couldn't get it together,' you know? So I try to make people feel like they can do it themselves." ✕

Annie Buckley is a Los Angeles-based artist and writer. Her essay "Lighting the Labyrinth: Marnie Weber's Spirit Song" was published in the catalog accompanying Weber's 2007 exhibition at Patrick Painter Gallery.

Photography by Marnie Weber, courtesy of Patrick Painter Gallery

Craft: **PROJECTS**

H ave a wardrobe that needs a lift? Learn to smith copper while creating gorgeous buttons, then design tessellation patterns to print onto tees and pants. But don't stop at the closet ... make macramé curtains with suede and beads to accessorize your pad, sew custom seat covers to punch up your car, and build a birdhouse to liven up your garden. Sprucing up has never been so fun!

Photograph by Jen Siska

RESTORATION HARDWARE

By Christine Haynes and Kent Bell

BRING A VINTAGE GARMENT BACK TO LIFE WITH CUSTOM METALWORK.

» The U.S. penny today is made out of zinc with only 2.5 grams of copper coating. From 1793 to 1837 pennies were pure copper.

▶▶ You've been there: you go to a vintage clothing store and find the ultimate score. But there's just one problem: it's missing a button. Dang it! Now what?

Rather than reach into the odd button bin for a quick fix, why not take this opportunity to create a one-of-a-kind masterpiece? In this project, learn to smith and form copper into a gorgeous floral button unlike anything else in your wardrobe.

» Copper and turquoise are widely used in traditional Native American jewelry.

Don't need a button? Don't despair. This project is easily adapted to customize a wide array of projects from accessories to jewelry. You can take the skills you learn here to create just about anything you can think of. And copper is just the beginning; metalsmithing opens up whole new worlds in jewelry-making and accessories.

» Women's blouses button from the left, the opposite of men's shirts, supposedly because 19th century Victorian women were dressed by right-handed maids and the reversal made it easier.

Designers Christine Haynes and Kent Bell combine their metalsmithing and sewing skills into their company, Twospace. See the fruit of their labors at twospace.com.

Photograph by Jen Siska at Idol Vintage, San Francisco; illustrations by Tim Lillis

WHAT YOU'LL NEED

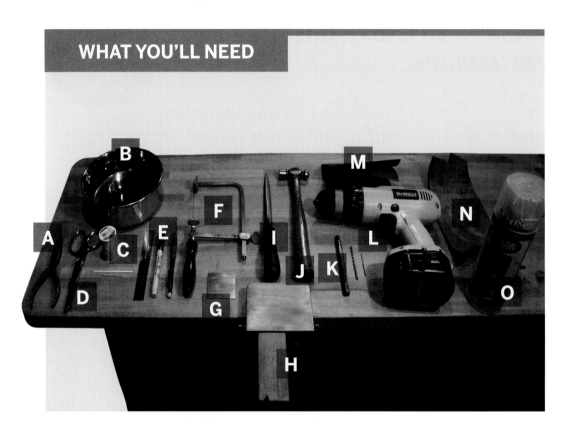

[A] Needlenose pliers

[B] Metal pot or pan with cold water

[C] Needle and thread

[D] Scissors

[E] Ruler, pencil, and felt-tipped permanent marker, thin tip preferred

[F] Jeweler's saw frame with #2 saw blades

[G] 2" square of 16-gauge (thick) copper

[H] Bench pin

[I] Fine-toothed metal file

[J] Small ball-peen hammer

[K] Center punch

[L] Drill and drill bits 1/16" and 1/8"

[M] Fine grit (400) wet/dry sandpaper

[N] Heavy piece of scrap leather

[O] Clear spray acrylic

[NOT SHOWN]
Gas stove
Oven mitts
Eye protection

Photography by Christine Haynes and Kent Bell

⏩ BOSS A CUSTOM COPPER BUTTON

Time: 1 Day Complexity: Medium

1. ANNEAL THE COPPER

Our project requires that the copper button be domed with a hammer into a three-dimensional form. Doing this is easiest when the copper is softened beforehand by a simple process called annealing.

1a. Before you begin, fill a metal pot or pan partway with cool water, and have it nearby. Use a pair of needlenose pliers to hold your piece of copper over a gas burner set on high, being careful to never place your hand over the burner. Gently hover the piece near the tips of the flames in a small circular motion so that no area receives more heat than another. You will notice the copper going through color changes as it heats, from its original hue, to a metallic rainbow, then a dark phase, and finally into a dull, glowing red. Turn off the lights to better see these color changes.

1b. Just as the metal is beginning to reach a dull red, drop it into the cool water to quench it.

👓 **SAFETY TIPS: Because the pliers themselves can get hot, be sure the handles are not covered by flammable materials, and be sure to protect your hands with fire-resistant oven mitts to avoid getting burned. Also, wear eye protection and be certain to avoid splashing the water or being scalded by the flash of steam when quenching. Some people are mildly allergic to inhaled copper fumes and dust; to avoid a reaction, work in a well-ventilated area. If annealing over a stove, use the stove's ventilation fan while heating the copper.**

- -

ALTERNATIVE METHODS: Any open flame can be used to anneal copper, provided it's hot enough. Contact with the flames of outdoor gas grills, campfires, and even charcoal grills can bring copper to annealing temperature (700°F). Gas torches are the most common heat source used by silversmiths, but they are not covered here due to myriad safety and preparation issues.

1c. After the piece is quenched, you will notice the metal is still discolored from oxidation. Several methods can be used to clean the oxides off the copper, including submerging the piece in a slightly acidic solution or "pickle."

For the purposes of this project, lightly sanding the copper with 400 grit wet/dry sandpaper will bring back the original shine of the copper without losing the softness gained through annealing.

2. PIERCE THE DISK

Cutting metal with a jeweler's saw is called piercing. A jeweler's saw is not unlike a stringed musical instrument. The tighter the tension on the blade, the more responsive and accurate the tool will be. A standard jeweler's saw frame has 3 setscrews — 2 that clamp the saw blade into place at each end and a third that sets the distance between the clamps.

2a. Set your saw blade. Begin by placing one end of your saw blade into one of the clamp screws. Be certain that the teeth of the blade are pointed outward and down toward the handle. Next, adjust the distance between the 2 clamp screws until the loose end of the saw blade barely overlaps the second clamp. Tighten the distance setscrew to this setting. Pressing one end against a workbench or doorjamb, squeeze or bow the saw frame so that the loose end of the saw blade can be held firmly by the second clamp. Once the last screw is set, let the frame spring apart and put tension on the blade. A properly set saw blade will make a high-pitched musical note when plucked. If it feels loose or does not "ring" a note, the blade is too loose and needs to be reset.

2b. Mark your piece. A can, bottle top, or compass can be used to draw a circle onto your metal with a thin-tipped permanent marker.

NOTE: If you're making a button for a vintage garment, be certain that your button is slightly smaller in diameter than the pre-existing buttonhole.

2c. Pierce your disk. Place your piece on the bench pin so that the cutting line is slightly over the right edge. A bench pin is a mounted piece of wood that extends out from your workbench. It's designed to provide a stable platform while allowing tool access to the work piece from nearly all directions.

Hold the piece down with your left hand, and hold the saw blade perpendicular to the piece. Cut into the metal with long, steady, lightly pressured strokes of the saw. When cutting around curves and corners, rather than turn the saw blade into the curve, it's easier to keep the saw position straight and consistent, and turn the piece being cut with your holding hand.

2d. Smooth the disk. Once the circle is cut, use a fine-toothed metal file to adjust the shape, correct any mistakes, round out sharp edges, and remove any unwanted burrs from the disk.

❋ **TIP: Practice piercing on a scrap piece of copper until you feel confident enough to move on to your real piece.**

🥽 **SAFETY TIP: To avoid injury, be sure to position your hands so that you are cutting or filing away from your fingers.**

3. BOSS THE BUTTON

After annealing, the copper is very soft and pliable, and can be shaped with the greatest of ease. First, you'll need to work on a nice solid surface, like a heavy bench top, cinder block, anvil, or butcher's block. Working on an unsupported surface will greatly reduce the efficiency of your work and create a lot of noise to boot.

You'll also need a small ball-peen hammer. Take time beforehand to file, sand, and polish the round end of the hammer so that no marks, gouges, or other surface imperfections are visible. A flawed or uneven peen can mark the surface of the copper with every hammer blow. A smooth, evenly shaped peen will transfer its polished surface to your piece. Finally, place a thick piece of leather between your disk and your workbench, as this surface will prevent scratching and marring and will also allow just enough "give" to shape your piece.

3a. Starting from the center, begin hammering the metal in short, even strokes. Be careful to use equal force with every blow and to move slowly and gradually around the surface. Each hammer blow will leave a mark, and each mark should slightly overlap the marks before it. You will notice that smithing the piece will "work-harden" the copper, meaning the areas you hammer will lose the pliability gained from annealing and return to a stiff, hard state.

3b. Gradually rotate the disk so that your hammer blows will spiral outward in concentric circles. As you move outward, you'll notice the center of the disk bending downward, and the edges of the disk raising up off the table. As you progress, be sure to tilt the piece so that the hammer strikes the copper at its lowest point, where the copper is in direct contact with the underlying leather. Continue spiraling outward until the entire surface is covered in hammer marks. Be consistent in your spacing, and in the force of your hammer blows, as inconsistencies will cause a lumpy, irregular form.

NOTE: There are countless methods for shaping and forming metal, and this project describes only bossing. To learn more about other silversmithing methods, we highly recommend Oppi Untracht's *Metal Techniques for Craftsmen* and Tim McCreight's *The Complete Metalsmith: An Illustrated Handbook*.

3c. Once you've completed your course of bossing, your piece is now formed into a shallow bowl. If it's not deep enough for your tastes, you can repeat Steps 1 and 3 to re-anneal and continue to boss the metal for a deeper bowl. The more courses of bossing, the deeper the bowl will be.

4. DRILL THE BUTTON

4a. Using your ruler, find the center of the bowl's interior surface. Mark 4 spots with your permanent marker around the center point of the bowl so that they form the 4 corners of a ¼" square.

4b. Lightly stamping your drilling spots with a center punch ensures that your holes will be drilled accurately, by giving the drill bit a natural divot in which to take hold. To mark the corners, place the point of your center punch on each corner and tap it lightly once with your hammer. Again, work from the inside of the piece and be certain that the back of the piece is touching your workbench when you strike the punch. This provides support and prevents denting or misshaping the piece.

👓 **SAFETY TIP: On occasion, the drill bit may seize in your piece and cause it to spin unexpectedly. Use leather work gloves to protect your hands and improve your grip. For larger drill bits and/or faster speeds, secure the piece with a clamp or vise and keep your hands away from the piece entirely.**

4c. Using the 1⁄16" drill bit, drill the 4 holes. You can use your bench pin or a piece of scrap wood so that you don't drill into your workbench once the bit goes through the metal.

4d. Once the holes are drilled, you may notice rough edges or burrs around the holes. Using just your fingers, twist a larger drill bit in the holes to shave off any excess material and bevel the edges so that they don't snag.

5. PIERCE DETAILS INTO YOUR FORM

Our design is inspired by lily pads and clovers, and to get the look we want, we need to cut our circular shape into something a little more organic.

Use your marker to draw the areas you need to remove. Using the same methods described in Step 2, pierce away the unwanted portions with your jeweler's saw. If cutting into a sharp corner, cut one line into the corner and back your saw out. Then cut in from the other direction to complete the corner. Use your file to finish and smooth out your final shape.

6. ADD SOME PATINA TO YOUR BUTTON

In Step 1, we saw copper go through a color change as it was heated. What we didn't tell you is that the copper can be quenched at any stage of the color shift to preserve the color properties.

6a. Begin by removing any fingerprints or other surface impurities. We are putting a lightly sanded or "brushed" finish on our button, but if you prefer the existing texture, you can use dish soap or other "degreasing" cleaners. Once the surface is cleaned, be certain that the piece is rinsed and dried thoroughly, and avoid any new contact with your fingers.

6b. As in Step 1, begin to slowly heat the copper. We don't want to heat it so much that it anneals; we're just looking for a rainbow that occurs at a much lower temperature. Be fast on your feet! The very moment you see a colorful pattern that appeals to you, quench the metal!

6c. To make the color permanent and prevent color change over time, spray both sides with 2 coats of acrylic clear coat. Some slight color change may occur. Do not overspray as this may cause drips, and remember to let each coat dry before turning the piece over or handling it.

7. SEW IT ON

For tips on sewing buttons onto this project and others, see craftzine.com/04/copperbutton.

FINISH ☒

▶▶ PROJECT ADAPTATIONS

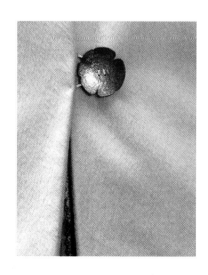

Chokers Use heavy velvet ribbon to create a beautiful choker. Sew the button on. Tie it on and wear it proudly.

Pendant necklaces Use the same velvet ribbon to make a pendant necklace. Make sure the length can fit over your head, as this design doesn't tie at the back. Bring the ends together so that the front face is facing forward on both ends, and pin. Sew the button through both ends at once.

Brooches Sew your button onto a 1½" piece of felt and use a safety pin to attach it to your favorite jacket.

Handbags and hats Replace the closure of a handbag, or embellish a hat.

BACKYARD BIRDHOUSE

By Joe Szuecs

HOME SWEET HOME FOR YOUR COMMON GARDEN BIRDS.

▶▶ Let's dispel a common misconception: birds do not need a little peg below the opening of a birdhouse. In fact, this design feature only helps egg-thieving predators. "But the birds at my mother's house perch on it!" Yes, they very well may do so. Fact is, they don't *need* it. They just zip right in and out of the opening.

This nesting box is designed to accommodate a few common backyard species: chickadee, titmouse, nuthatch, and wren. Of these, the chickadee is the most likely to rear its young in your handmade house, which is a very simple, functional design that's easy to build. The big fun comes when you decorate it. So while you're at it, build a bunch of them, invite your friends over, and have a birdhouse decorating party!

» The marsh wren spends hours crafting his own courtship nest. Once he's done, he starts on a brand new one.

» In the final attack scene of Alfred Hitchcock's 1963 movie *The Birds*, live birds were attached to the clothes of actress Tippi Hedren by nylon threads to prevent them from flying away.

» "Birdhouse in Your Soul" was one of the biggest hits of the 90s for alternative rock band They Might Be Giants.

Joe Szuecs, pronounced *sooch*, lives in western Sonoma County, Calif., and owns Renga Arts, a store that sells products made from recycled and reclaimed materials. rengaarts.com

Photography by Joe Szuecs; Illustrations by Tim Lillis

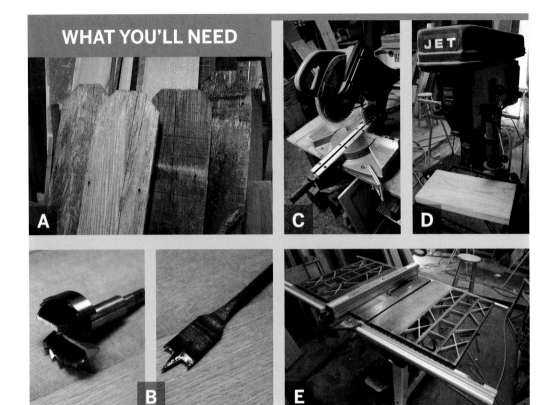

WHAT YOU'LL NEED

[A] 1"×6" redwood or cedar fence board 6' long

[B] 1⅛" Forstner bit or spade bit

[C] Miter saw (power recommended)

[D] Drill (power recommended)

[E] Table saw with dado blade

[NOT SHOWN]

Hammer

Large washer 1⅛" inner diameter

Paint or other materials for decorating

[FOR ALTERNATIVE BASE DESIGN]

1¼" brads (a package)

1½" brads (2)

1½" wood screw (1)

📷 See photos from the nest boxes we monitor in the orchard behind the offices of CRAFT: craftzine.com/go/nestboxes

The dimensions of a birdhouse, or nesting box, are very important. I'm always amazed at the preposterous location of the opening on those gift shop jobs. A given bird species demands a certain opening diameter and offset, inner layout, and hanging height. So before you fashion a nesting box out of that old fruit crate, make sure you target a certain bird and figure out the suitable measurements. If you're targeting a bird not mentioned in the intro, check out the measurement chart on the last page of this project.

►► BUILD AND DESIGN A CLASSIC NESTING BOX

Time: 2–3 Hours Complexity: Easy

1. SELECT A NICE PIECE OF WOOD

OK, you could jump in the car and zip over to the building supply superstore and purchase a nice new piece of wood. But that's for chumps. This classic woodworking project is all about appreciating the inherent beauty in a plank headed for the kindling pile. Needless to say, I have a few suggestions.

Weathered fence boards. You're familiar with old boards that have weathered to that distinctive shade of gray. I try to find fence pickets that have exaggerated grain patterns — the result of being pounded by the elements. Now, a caveat: Carefully inspect reclaimed boards for signs of rot and deep cracks, usually found where the pickets were in contact with the fence rails. You need to find a good solid 4' section. When tapped with your knuckle, it should sound solid.

Old painted boards. Barn red is the most popular color here, closely followed by white. The more signs of age, the better. If you're really lucky, you'll find boards that have been painted multiple times with different colors, where the top layers are worn, letting lower layers show through.

NOTE: Generally speaking, the older the painted wood, the better. Unfortunately, before the 1970s, lead was a common ingredient in most paints. It's bad for you and bad for the birds. You can (and should) purchase an inexpensive lead test kit at your local hardware store before using painted wood of a questionable age.

2. CUT THE PIECES, THEN THE TRICKY BOTTOM SLOT

2a. Cut your boards according to the dimensions in the diagram on the following page.

2b. This design provides a removable bottom to make cleaning easy. The bottom piece simply slips into a slot in the back slat and is secured with a single screw. Fantastic. Unfortunately, without a router or table saw dado blade, cutting the slot is a pain, but not impossible. If you have the equipment, cut the slot as shown, and move on to Step 3.

You can also use the 2-brad design (see diagram on following page). Drive two 1½" brads into the back edge of the base piece until ¾" remains exposed. Later on, you'll simply drill 2 holes into the back piece. The protruding brads will slide into the holes, and the base will be secured by a single screw.

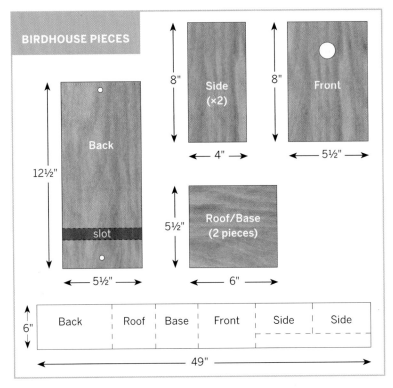

BIRDHOUSE PIECES

Side (×2)   8"   4"

Front   8"   5½"

Back   12½"   5½"   slot

Roof/Base (2 pieces)   5½"   6"

Back   Roof   Base   Front   Side   Side   6"   49"

Back: 5½"×12½"
Front: 5½" × 8"
Side (×2): 4"×8"
Roof: 5½"×6"
Base: 5½"×6"

**NOTE: Pay attention
to the direction of
the grain reflected
in the diagram.**

3. DRILL SOME HOLES

3a. Using the 1⅛" bit, drill the birdhouse's opening, centered 2" from the top edge of the front panel.
I recommend using a Forstner bit because it creates a nice, clean hole. An auger bit is an acceptable substitute.

3b. Using a ¼" bit, drill the mounting holes into the back panel. Optionally, you can drill a few drain holes
into the base.

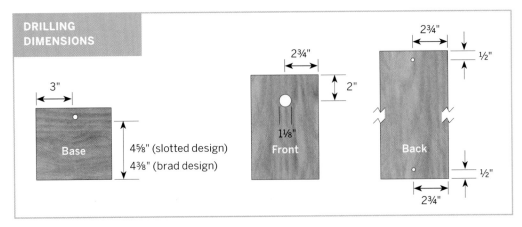

**DRILLING
DIMENSIONS**

Base   3"   4⅝" (slotted design)   4⅜" (brad design)

Front   2¾"   2"   1⅛"

Back   2¾"   ½"   ½"   2¾"

4. NAIL IT TOGETHER AND ATTACH THE BOTTOM

4a. Nail it together as per the diagram.

4b. For the slotted design, simply drill a small hole into the base ¾" from the front edge. Position the base in the slot and attach with a 1½" wood screw.

4c. For the brad design, nail a 1½" brad into the back edge of the base, 1½" from the side. Leave ¾" of the brad sticking out. Repeat on the same edge, at the other end.

Align the base on the bottom of the box, the 2 brads in contact with the box's back board. Push the bottom against the back board to make 2 marks with the brads. Drill 2 holes, a little wider in diameter than the brads, at these marks. The base should fit nicely into these holes. Attach with a 1½" wood screw.

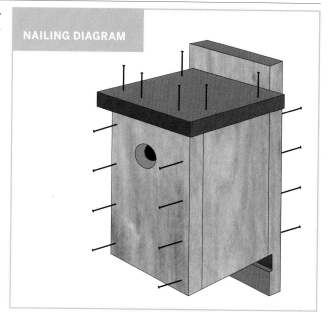

NAILING DIAGRAM

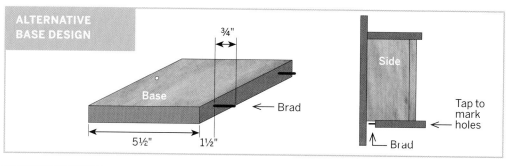

ALTERNATIVE BASE DESIGN

¾"

Base

Brad

5½"   1½"

Side

Tap to mark holes

Brad

5. INSTALL THE WOODPECKER RING

What is this for? Woodpeckers like to peck out the holes of nesting boxes. This never leads to them using the box — just makes it unsuitable for the target species. A metal ring installed around the opening prevents this.

5a. The easiest thing to use is a large metal washer with a 1⅛" inner diameter opening. Drill 2 holes in the washer, position over the entrance hole in the box, and secure with a couple of screws.

5b. Alternatively, you can fashion a metal ring out of tin — a flattened can is great. Cut a 3"-diameter disk. Mark a 1⅛" circle in the center. Cut the disk in half. Now cut out the inner half circles, carefully following the marks. Simply nail the 2 halves, using small-headed tacks, around the box opening.

6. PAINT, DECORATE, AND HANG YOUR HOUSE

At this point, you have a fully functional birdhouse. There are infinite options for decoration. A simple coat of paint, perhaps. Designs with copper sheeting, twigs, or other materials. Here are a few of my designs to help inspire you.

When you're ready, I recommend that you hang your birdhouse about 6' off the ground. At that height, it's easier to reach the box opening for cleaning. For more details on hanging heights for specific birds, refer to the chart on the opposite page.

  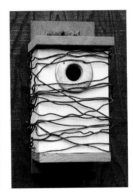 

FINISH ☒

AFTER THE FACT

» PLACING YOUR BOX

Cavity-nesting birds are very particular about where they live. No matter how perfect your nest box, if you don't have the right habitat, the birds aren't likely to find it. Luckily, titmice, wrens, and chickadees are very common and pretty easy to attract. By putting out a bird feeder and birdbath, you can easily increase the number and variety of birds that frequent your yard, thereby increasing the chances of occupation.

You can hang your birdhouse on a tree, on a fence, or on a pole. The birdhouses I've designed have 2 mounting holes that make it simple to screw into a tree or fence post. Screws can damage some trees, so if you have both, pick the fence post. Metal poles are great because they make it much harder for predators, like snakes and raccoons, to raid the nest. Of course, it's a lot more work to install a pole.

Don't hang the birdhouse on the side of your house or garage. There's probably too much activity

in these areas to encourage nesting. Give your birds a little space and privacy! Similarly, it's a bad idea to put a birdhouse too close to a bird feeder.

Birds nest in the spring. Make sure your birdhouse is hung by late February or early March in warmer climates. April to early May is fine in northern areas.

» CARING FOR YOUR BIRDHOUSE

Birds don't like to nest in boxes that have already been used. After the babies have left the nest, you should clean it out. Watch the box for a week or so. If you don't see any activity, go up to the box and tap it. No sounds? Carefully unscrew the bottom and remove it. Simply pull out all remnants of the nest. Reattach the bottom, and, with luck, another pair of birds may nest later that same year.

In the fall, you can leave the house out or bring it inside for the winter. If you do leave it out, you should clean it again after the winter weather lets up.

Source: "Homes for Birds," U.S. Fish & Wildlife Service, Office of Migratory Bird Management. craftzine.com/go/birds

NEST BOX DIMENSIONS

Species	Box floor (inches)	Box height (inches)	Entrance height from base (inches)	Entrance hole diameter (inches)	Placement height from ground (feet)
American robin*	7×8	8	—	—	6–15
Eastern & western bluebird	5×5	8–12	6–10	1½	4–6
Mountain bluebird	5×5	8–12	6–10	1½	4–6
Chickadee	4×4	8–10	6–8	1⅛	4–15
Titmice	4×4	10–12	6–10	1¼	5–15
Ash-throated flycatcher	6×6	8–12	6–10	1½	5–15
Phoebe*	6×6	6	—	—	8–12
Brown-headed pygmy nuthatch, red-breasted nuthatch	4×4	8–10	6–8	1¼	5–15
Prothonotary warbler	5×5	6	4–5	1⅛	4–8
Barn swallow*	6×6	6	—	—	8–12
Purple martin	6×6	6	1–2	2¼	6–20
Tree swallow, violet-green swallow	5×5	6–8	4–6	1½	5–15
Downy woodpecker	4×4	8–10	6–8	1¼	5–15
Hairy woodpecker	6×6	12–15	9–12	1½	8–20
Lewis' woodpecker	7×7	16–18	14–16	2½	12–20
Northern flicker	7×7	16–18	14–16	2½	6–20
Red-headed woodpecker	6×6	12–15	9–12	2	10–20
Yellow-bellied sapsucker	5×5	12–15	9–12	1½	10–20
Bewick's wren, house wren	4×4	6–8	4–6	1¼	5–10
Barn owl	10×18	15–18	4	6	12–18
Screech owl and American kestrel (sparrow hawk)	8×8	12–15	9–12	3	10–30
Wood duck	10×18	10–24	12–16	4	10–20
A. Red-tailed hawk, great-horned owl B. Osprey	**A.** 24"×24" platform / **B.** 48"×48" platform				

*** Use nesting shelf, which is a platform with three sides and an open front.**

MODERN MACRAMÉ CURTAIN

By Cathi Milligan

GET KNOTTY WITH SUEDE AND BEADS.

▶▶ Macramé, the art of decorating with knots, can be traced back to the 13th century, when it was created by Arabs. Excess thread was knotted along the edges of fabric to create fringe and decoration. Through conquest and trade, the craft of macramé worked its way around the world.

But what most people think of when they hear the word "macramé" are those plant holders made out of jute from the 70s. Macramé is so much more than that! There's jewelry and belts and curtains, and yes, even plant holders.

This project uses simple knots, supple suede lace, and sparkling beads to create a very modern macramé beaded curtain that will make any doorway or window fabulous!

» On *The Brady Bunch* episode "A Room at the Top" (1973), Greg Brady finally gets his own room in the attic. Greg transforms it into a 70s-style bachelor pad, complete with beaded doorway.

» Cavandoli macramé creates geometric patterns through techniques similar to weaving.

» North American sailors long ago used to spend many hours using macramé to make netting, screens, and fringes for wheels and bell covers during long months at sea.

Cathi Milligan is an L.A.-based crafter who dabbles in many mediums, including glass bead-making and macramé. She's been seen on DIY Network's *Jewelry Making* and *Craft Lab* demonstrating some of her fine crafts. beadbrains.com

Photograph by Carrie Hannegan; illustrations by Tim Lillis

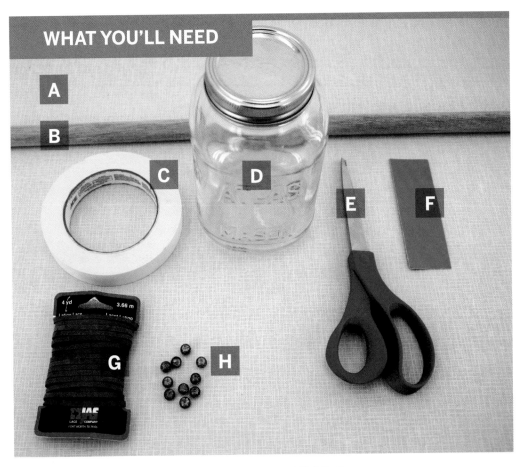

WHAT YOU'LL NEED

A B C D E F G H

TO MAKE THE 3'×6' MACRAMÉ CURTAIN

[A] A 3'×6' macramé board or a large table

[B] Curtain rod

[C] Masking tape

[D] Small glass jar

[E] Scissors

[F] Card stock for bobbins

[G] Suede lace 400 yds

[H] Beads (200–300) of varied size, shape, and color I used glass beads, but any beads will work.
NOTE: The hole in the bead must be big enough to accommodate 2 or 4 strands of the suede.

[NOT SHOWN]

Finials (optional) if you are making your own curtain rod

Epoxy (optional) to attach finials

TO BUILD A 3'×6' MACRAMÉ BOARD (OPTIONAL)

½" plywood, 4'×8' sheet You'll cut two 3'×3' pieces for the macramé board, then use the leftover pieces (1'×6' and 2'×4') to make a stand for the board.

Saw

Hammer and nails

Wood filler

Sandpaper

Primer and paint

Paintbrushes/rollers

Paper rulers (8) trimmed to fit

Double-sided tape

Clear acrylic paint

Clear varnish spray

Pencil

Piano hinge with screws

Vinyl-coated hooks (2) to hold curtain rod

Hacksaw or handheld rotary power tool with cut-off blade such as a Dremel

Power screwdriver

Photograph by Sam Murphy

KNOT A SUEDE MACRAMÉ CURTAIN

Time: 2–3 Weeks Complexity: Easy

1. MAKE YOUR MACRAMÉ BOARD (OPTIONAL)

Most macramé projects are done on 12"×18" boards made of a soft particleboard, but this project requires a larger board, 3'×6', made of plywood. You can also do this project on a large table, but the macramé board lets you see how everything is hanging. If you choose to use a table, go to Step 2.

1a. Cut two 3'×3' pieces of plywood, and fill the crevices with wood filler. Sand the board twice before priming the surface. Two coats of primer are sufficient, and then 2 coats of paint. Good attention to the board now will prevent your suede from snagging when you're working.

1b. On one side of each board, attach paper rulers to all 4 edges with double-sided tape, and seal with clear acrylic paint. Draw a grid with a pencil in 1" increments, then seal with clear spray. The grid assists quite a bit in measuring the spaces between knots.

1c. Connect the 2 boards with a piano hinge that has been cut down to size. A hand power tool with cut-off blades works well; you can also use a hacksaw. Wear eye protection. Screw in vinyl-coated hooks at the top 2 corners to hold the curtain rod.

1d. Use the leftover plywood to make a stand for the board. Trim the 1'×6' piece to make an upright measuring 54" tall, 11½" wide at the bottom, and 9" wide at the top, tapering on just one side. This creates a slight angle that allows the board to lean back while hanging on the stand. Attach the upright to a 1'×1' base, cut from the remaining scrap. Sandwich 2 wood strips around the bottom of the upright (mine measured 1½"×11½"×½"), then drive nails through them all to attach the base securely.

Hold the macramé board against the upright at the height that you'll want to work. Where the top of the upright meets the board, nail 3 small pieces of wood in an upside-down U shape as shown, so the board can be slipped onto the stand and hang there. I put hand weights on the base behind the board to hold everything in place.

Photography by Cathi Milligan

2. PREP YOUR CURTAIN ROD

All macramé projects require the material to be mounted on something for support. That something can be cord, rings, or in the case of this project, a curtain rod. I used a 36" piece of decorative wrought iron for my curtain rod. It was cut from a 10' piece, which yielded three 3' pieces and a 1' practice piece.

2a. Lightly sand your curtain rod to smooth any sharp or rough edges. Thoroughly clean it afterward.

2b. Attach finials with epoxy to the ends of the rod to keep the project from slipping off during transport.

3. CALCULATE HOW MUCH SUEDE AND BEADS YOU'LL NEED

For most macramé projects, you'll need anywhere from 1½ to 8 times the finished length in material, depending on the complexity of your knots and designs. How big are your beads? The longer the beads, the more space they use. All of this plays into your material requirements. The knots for this project are simple. They are repeated in each section and alternated. Each section will have either overhand knots, or a combination of square knots and twist knots. The overhand knot uses all 4 strands for both the knots and the bead stringing, while the square and twist knots use the 2 inside strands as holding strands and the 2 outside as working strands. The holding strands will be used for stringing beads.

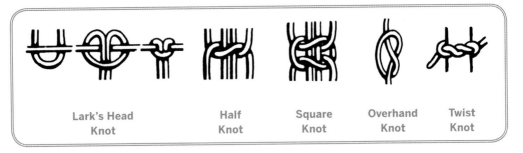

| Lark's Head Knot | Half Knot | Square Knot | Overhand Knot | Twist Knot |

3a. A leftover piece of curtain rod is perfect to practice a few knots and to get an idea of how much material will be required for this project. Cut four 2'-long strands of your suede lace. Mount one on the rod using the lark's head knot, folding it in half and looping over the rod. This yields 2 strands. Do this twice to create a section, giving you 4 strands per section. Create 2 sections and measure across. Space the sections out and see how they look. Each section measures approximately ⅜", and with about ¾" between them, 30 sections will work well.

3b. To estimate your length needs, give yourself too much suede lace and embark on your most complicated set of knots, then see how much lace is left over. It's best to figure this out first so you don't run short of materials at the end of a section. For the most complicated section, which included more knots and less space between those knots, I used about 24' (×2) per section, or 48' (16 yds). The pattern I used was: square knot, bead, square knot, space (1¼"), twist knot (8 knots), space (1¼"), square knot, bead, square knot, and repeat. The more knots used, the more materials used.

3c. Organize your beads, noting most importantly the hole size. Bead size is important too, but you need holes big enough to fit 2 or 4 strands through. (I make my own beads, but you don't have to make your own to create a fabulous curtain. Check your local bead or craft stores, or go online. Take samples of your material with you if you need to.)

Take your practice strands and tape 2 strands together, then 4 strands together, so you can test bead hole size and organize your beads accordingly.

4. MOUNT YOUR SECTIONS

4a. Hang your board up on the stand and place the curtain rod on the hooks. It's also possible to do this project on a big table — it's up to you. When the board is on the stand you can see how everything is hanging, but you have to contend with gravity while making your knots. It can be a bit like juggling.

Place a spool of suede lace in a small glass jar while pulling out the amounts you'll need for each strand and section. The jar will contain the spool and keep the lace from running away.

4b. Start by mounting your sections anywhere on the rod. I find that the design evolves as you add more to it. To mount the sections that will be made up of overhand knots, measure out about 20' of suede lace. Fold the lace in half and loop it over the rod, then bring the 2 strands through the loop and tighten. This is the lark's head knot used to mount the sections. Repeat with another piece so that your section will have 4 strands total to work with. Trim the ends even, then tape the 4 ends together to make it easier to string beads.

Use a piece of card stock as a bobbin, and cut it strategically to lock the lace in once it's rolled up. Roll it up to a more manageable length. You'll unroll it as needed.

4c. To mount the sections that use square knots and twist knots, use the same amount of lace, about 20', but mount it a bit differently. The square knots and twist knots have inside holding strands that don't require extra material, but their outside working strands need more material than the overhand knots. So, when folding the strands over to loop onto the rod, make sure the inside holding strands (just a bit longer than the finished length) are shorter than the outside strands (which should be at least double the finished length). This saves quite a bit of material.

4d. Once both strands for a section are mounted, take the 2 inside holding strands, trim the ends evenly, and tape the 2 ends together so it's easier to string beads. Take the outside working strands and wrap each onto a card-stock bobbin to a manageable length. The inside holding strands need to be taped to the board so that the working strands can knot around them. Tape these down, about 6" below where the knots will go. You'll remove the tape whenever you add beads, and you'll have to replace the tape now and then as it loses its stickiness.

4e. Don't mount too many sections at a time — it can be quite a bit to wrangle. Starting with a couple of sections allows you to go back and forth without getting yourself all tangled up. The design in this curtain relies quite a bit on space between knots and beads. This uses less material than a densely knotted section. Varied sections add texture and interest and give the viewer more to look at.

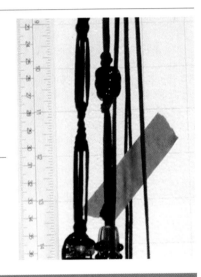

5. START KNOTTING

5a. Start your first knot 1" or so from the rod. It's your design choice whether to add beads immediately or in the next knot down. The knots trap the beads and hold them in place. A pattern of knots for the overhand sections could be: knot, space (2"), knot, bead, knot, space (2"), and repeat.

5b. For the sections using square and twist knots, the material is handled a little bit differently. **A square knot is built by making 2 half knots, one the reverse of the other; this creates the square. To achieve the twist, the half knots are continued in the same direction; I find it's best to do at least 8 knots to get a good twist.** You can see why these sections require more material. Also remember to tighten each knot well, but don't tug too hard since the suede can break if pulled too forcefully. When you want to thread a bead, you'll free the inside strands from their tape, string the bead on, then replace the tape to hold those strands down on the board.

5c. Back to knotting. Patterns can be similar to those used with the overhand knots: square knot, space (1"), twist knot (8 knots), space (1"), square, bead, square, space (2"), repeat. This is a design suggestion; you can use the piece of practice rod to work out other combinations you might use. You can also practice the knots by making belts or jewelry.

6. WATCH THE DESIGN TAKE SHAPE

As you complete more sections, you can decide where you might want to knot sections that have more space than beads and knots, or more beads and knots than space. Try different combinations of knots. On some of my sections I've used smaller beads, while on others I've chosen longer beads. And most of the sections have a fine blend of colors, styles, and sizes.

»**Beads:** The beads I make are known as lampworked, torched, or wound beads and are created on a steel rod known as a mandrel. It's the mandrel that gives the bead its hole. Glass is heated at a torch until it is molten, and then is wound around the mandrel. Once cooled, the finished bead can then be removed. This is the same way beads have been made for centuries.

NOTE: For more info on glass bead making, go to **beadbrains.com**.

7. TRIM AND HANG

7a. As you finish each section, trim the ends close to the floor. I like to trim a little long at first, since you can go back once the curtain is finished and even everything up. Once all the sections are complete, do a finished trim. Also consider varying the lengths at the bottom.

7b. To hang your finished curtain, you'll need hooks attached to the doorway or window where your magnificent piece of fine craft will be displayed. Or mount it out from the wall or hang it from the ceiling, as a room divider. (Mounting hardware is available at most hardware stores.)

This is a fun project that is very Zen-like in its repetitiveness. And the finished piece is worth the effort.

FINISH ☒

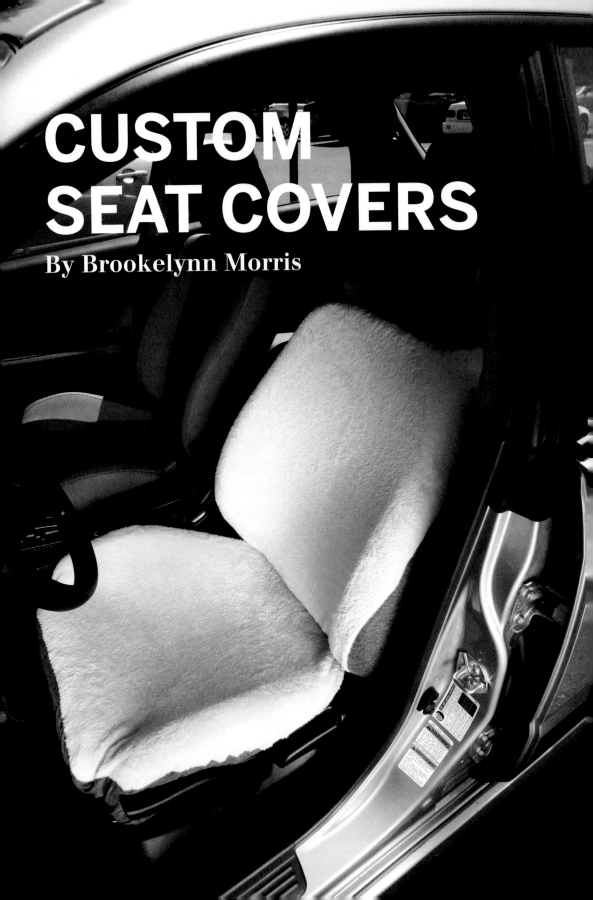

CUSTOM SEAT COVERS

By Brookelynn Morris

DESIGN AND SEW ORIGINAL, COZY COVERS FOR YOUR RIDE.

» The MTV show *Pimp My Ride* gives old cars new facelifts by tricking them out with new paint, fancy wheels, and as many flat-screen monitors as they can fit inside.

▶▶ Car seats get dirty. Some get filthy, even. Mud, coffee, the dog's winter coat: they all reduce the best car to the worst mess. Fight the filth, and make something that's clean, creative, and cozy. Give new life to the upholstery, while adding comfort and style. Regardless of what shape your seats are in, you can spend the afternoon crafting an answer.

Basic sewing skills combine with common-sense pattern building to create this custom seat cover. Simple materials are used, including stretchy jersey, soft, furry fleece, and big industrial snaps. The resulting project has form and function: a seat cover that looks just right and works even better. Someone call the dog, it's time to go to the beach!

» Four million cabbies can't be wrong! Wooden bead seat covers not only promote air flow, the gentle massage action of the beads increases circulation by removing concentrated pressure points.

» CritBuns is a portable foam seat, developed by Joe Gebbia, a former design student who developed the product after hours of sitting on cold, hard furniture and floors during art critiques.

Brookelynn Morris hates pronouns, but she loves you. Writing is her favorite. That, and figuring out how to do something she has never done before. brookelynn23.com

Photograph by Sam Murphy; illustrations by Tim Lillis

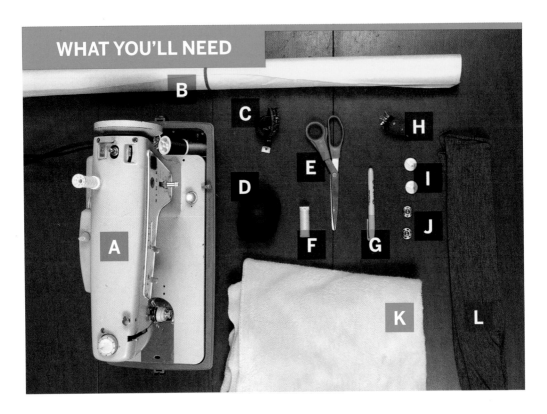

WHAT YOU'LL NEED

[A] Sewing machine

[B] Butcher paper (6'–10')

[C] Tape measure

[D] 1" wide elastic
(a few feet)

[E] Scissors

[F] Thread

[G] Marker

[H] Straight pins, needles
Shown here in a felted straw-
berry pin cushion, handmade
by Brookelynn. Check out
craftzine.com/02/needle_
felt for more fab
felting projects.

[I] Decorative buttons or
pins to cover snaps

[J] Large snaps (2)

[K] Fabric for front of seat
cover (2yds) Furry is fun!

[L] Fabric for back of seat
cover (1½yds) Stretchy is
essential.

NOTE: These material
measurements reflect
amounts used for the car
seats pictured here. Since
you'll be making your
very own pattern, your
measurements may vary.
Also, the amount of stretch
a fabric has affects the
yardage you'll need.
Be free and experiment!

⚠ **WARNING: Do not
put seat covers on seats
that have airbags inside
them. The covers could
impede the function of
the air bag system.**

Photography by Nat Wilson-Heckathorn

⏩ PATTERN AND SEW YOUR OWN ONE-OF-A-KIND SEAT COVERS

Time: 2–4 Hours Complexity: **Medium**

1. CHOOSE THE FABRIC AND GATHER SUPPLIES

Let style be your guide when selecting fabric for this project, but don't forget that cars are heavy traffic areas. Fake fur is fun, but the long fibers can be difficult to keep clean. This example uses a shaggy fleece with nice texture and a short pile. The slight stretch helps keep the fit snug, the color works with the existing upholstery, and best of all, it's machine washable. Thin, extra-stretchy jersey is essential for the skirt at the bottom and the rear of the seat cover. The more give this fabric has, the better. And as with all fabric, wash and dry according to instructions *before* cutting and sewing.

2. TAKE MEASUREMENTS

2a. Measure the length of the seat back, from its top front edge, down to the seat, and through the crevice. Push the tape measure all the way through the crevice to the back.

❊ TIP: If both front seats are the same, work with the passenger seat only. The steering wheel just gets in the way.

2b. Measure the width of the front side of the seat back, at its widest point. Be sure to press the measuring tape flat along the curves of the seat to get an accurate number.

2c. Measure the width of the rear side of the seat back, from the edge of one wing to the edge of the other. Make sure this is the widest point. Measure the length also, from the top edge to the bottom crevice (this step not shown).

2d. For the seat bottom, measure the length from the back of the crevice to the front edge where the seat ends. Also measure the width at the widest point.

3. DRAW THE SEATS (3 PIECES)

3a. Begin with the seat bottom. Cut enough paper to cover the seat, but not so much that it's hard to fit inside the car. Lay the paper out flat against the seat. Smoosh the paper down inside the crevice, and make sure it stays there. Mark along the crevice and along the angle where the seat curves out.

3b. Working slowly, trace the outermost edge of the seat bottom. It's easy for the marker to get off track, so lift the paper to check the course often. If necessary, draw a new line and keep tracing. Just draw the half of the seat that you can see from outside the car. The inside edge is the same as the outside edge. Instead of trying to draw along the interior, fold and cut the paper for symmetry in Step 4.

3c. To draw the front side of the seat back, first remove the headrest, and then follow the same process as for the seat bottom. Smooth out the paper, and trace down the outer-most edge. Begin at the top of the seat where the headrest was. There might be an existing seam that's a good guideline. Adjust the tracing as needed, and again, only draw the outside half of the seat.

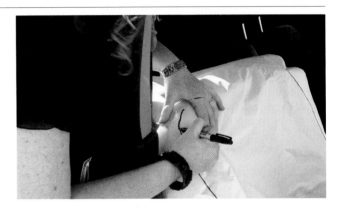

3d. To draw the rear side of the seat back, hop into the back seat. It can be difficult to trace this part of the seat. Trace along the top of the seat, referencing the same line as the front piece. Follow that seam with the marker, drawing out the width and the curved edges. Be certain that the widest points are drawn, and that the front and back pieces look like they will fit together.

4. MAKE THE PATTERNS

4a. Now you can easily make patterns from your drawings and measure-ments. For the seat bottom, take the paper and fold it in half lengthwise, so that the width from the edge of the pattern to the fold equals half the width of the entire seat bottom.

4b. Cut along the lines through both sides of the paper. When you unfold your pattern, you will have a perfectly symmetrical shape with measurements to match your seat. Repeat the process for the front and rear of the seat back.

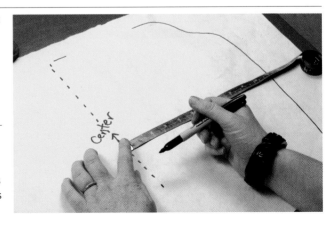

4c. Now take these 3 patterns and put them onto the seat. Confirm that they are exactly as desired. Check that the edges are even. Make sure the paper patterns have room to fit through the seat crevice to the other side. If necessary, trim down the edges, or adjust the shape on a new sheet of paper.

5. LAY OUT AND CUT THE FABRIC

5a. Trace and cut the seat bottom first. If the furry fabric you chose has a bit of stretch, lay out the fabric so the stretch runs side-to-side, not front-to-back. It is important that the bottom has the stretch going with the width. Pin the pattern in a few places and, giving yourself a generous seam allowance, trace around the pattern and then cut the fabric.

5b. For the front of the seat back, lay out the furry fabric with the stretch running vertically, so that the stretch goes with the length of the piece. Pin the fabric, trace while leaving a seam allowance, and cut.

5c. The rear of the seat back is next. Lay out the jersey so that the stretch goes with the width of the pattern, horizontally. This is the fabric with the most stretch; it's what allows the cover to stretch enough to fit on the seat, and it helps keep the cover nice and taut. Pin, trace, and cut out this last pattern piece. Check the cut-out fabric pieces against the seat.

6. SEW THE SKIRT

To make the lower skirt that covers the base of the seat, use a long strip of the jersey fabric. The length of this piece is determined by the distance around the outside edge of the seat bottom, the perimeter. The width should be about 6", and can be trimmed later.

6a. With the right sides facing in, pin the edge of the skirt fabric to the edge of the furry seat bottom fabric. Start at the point where the seat bottom fabric appears from under the crevice, and pin all around the edge to the opposite side.

6b. Sew this seam with a machine set to the widest zigzag setting. With the furry fleece I used, it was not necessary to change out the needle or foot, but different lengths of fur could require some mods to the machine.

6c. Back at the car, put the seat bottom/skirt on the seat to check the seams and fit. Pin where any excess jersey might need to be trimmed. I made this example with overkill, so quite a bit needed to be cut down.

7. SEW THE ELASTIC TO THE SKIRT

For this part of the project, it's essential to experiment with the placement of the elastic, the tension of the elastic, and the desired coverage from the skirt. One attempt with a piece of elastic that was too long produced a baggy and ill-fitting look. A second try with a shorter length was perfect. The shorter, tighter elastic pulled the jersey forward and upward, exposing the seat adjustment levers, but also keeping the seat cover down snugly.

7a. To sew the elastic, clamp the fabric and the elastic down with the foot of the sewing machine. Leave a tail of elastic to pull on. Stretch the elastic firmly, and stitch with a zigzag down the lower edge of the skirt. The fabric will ruffle and gather up.

7b. Take another trip to the car and assess the fit and performance of the seat bottom. In this example, to avoid an ugly edge and unsightly crooked sewing, the whole thing was tucked underneath itself. Looks great, doesn't it?

8. SEW THE REAR TO THE FRONT OF THE SEAT BACK

8a. Lay the facing sides of the fabrics for the seat back together. The rear jersey piece will be bigger than the front furry piece, so match them as carefully as possible. The seam ought to be smooth and well aligned.

8b. Begin pinning from the top center, near the headrest. Work down one side, and then down the other. Leave the last couple inches of each side, and the bottom edges, open. Sew these pieces together using the trusty zigzag. Hurry out to the car and see if it fits.

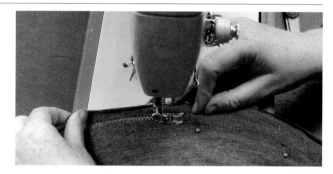

9. MARK AND ADD THE SEAM, SNAPS, AND HOLES FOR THE HEADREST

9a. Put both pieces of the seat cover onto the seat. Tug the edges through the crevice of the seat; climb into the back seat to line everything up. The seat bottom and the front of the seat back should be hanging out.

9b. With a marker or pins, mark the seam where the furry top and furry seat bottom will be sewn together. Now pull the rear piece of jersey down to the crevice. Line up points where the rear of the seat cover will snap to the edge of the seat bottom. Mark those spots and return to the sewing machine.

9c. Sew the 2 pieces together with the machine, along the seam marking. This will help keep the cover from shifting too much.

9d. With a needle and thread, sew the snaps in place. The top of the snap is sewn to the back of the jersey, and the bottom of the snap is sewn to the back of the fur. Follow any directions on the packaging for the snaps. They can be a test of patience. Cover the stitching with a fun button or pin.

9e. When the entire seat cover sits properly, and is snapped in perfectly, mark the holes for putting the headrest back into the seat. Cut these holes and hem them either by hand or by machine, using the buttonhole stitch.

You're done. Call the dog, grab your board, and get dirty!

FINISH

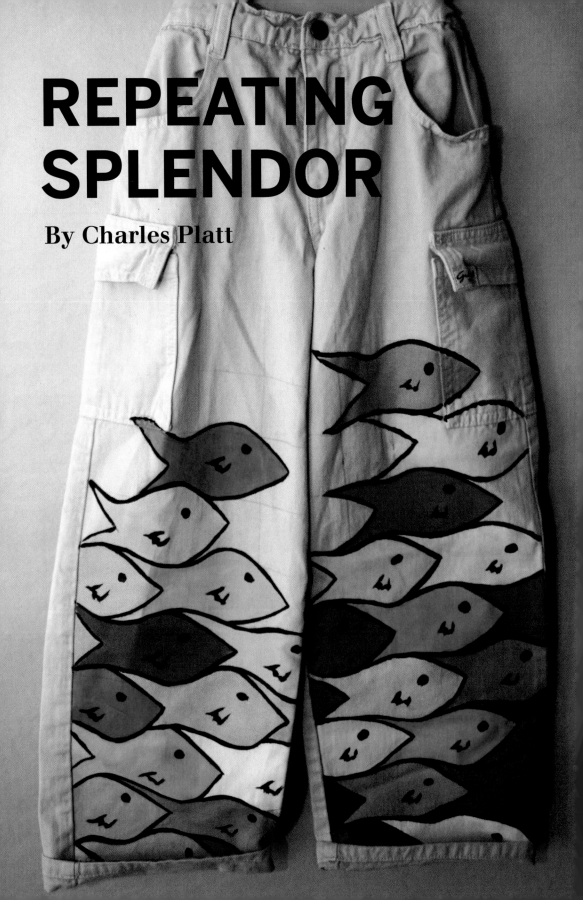

REPEATING SPLENDOR

By Charles Platt

DESIGN FABRIC WITH INTERLOCKING SHAPES AND PATTERNS.

>> Tessellations are among the oldest and simplest forms of decoration ever invented, and can be extremely beautiful. The word describes the art of dividing a surface into a pattern that repeats itself without leaving any gaps. Examples occur everywhere from stained glass windows to mosaic tiling to the interlocking patio bricks that you find at Home Depot. Even the squares on a checkerboard constitute a tessellation.

The graphic artist M.C. Escher used tessellations to depict interlocking silhouettes of animals, insects, and imaginary creatures. Despite their amazing complexity, even his most ambitious works were still based on an underlying geometrical grid — and so this is where we start.

Photography by Sam Murphy; illustrations by Tim Lillis; pants hand-painted by Lindsey North

» Dutch artist M.C. Escher was famous for his tessellation art, having created hundreds of tessellating shapes in the form of fish, birds, crabs, dogs, insects, people, and more.

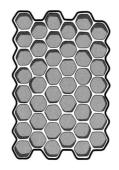

» A bee's honeycomb is a perfect example of tessellation in nature.

» The Alhambra palace in Granada, Spain, uses arabesque tessellations with an intricate pattern of leaves, flowers, vines, and calligraphy carved into the marble walls.

Charles Platt once majored in mathematics, and is now a section editor of MAKE magazine (**makezine.com**).

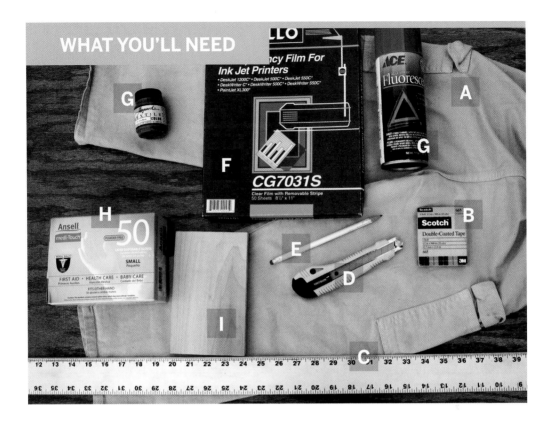

MATERIALS

[A] Fabric or T-shirt

[B] Double-sided tape

[C] Long straightedge such as a yardstick

[D] X-Acto knife

[E] Dressmaker's pencil

[F] Plastic film sold for use with an overhead projector

[G] Spray paint or fabric paint

[H] Thin rubber or latex gloves

[I] Wood or linoleum blocks (optional)

[NOT SHOWN]

Rag soaked in mineral spirits (optional)

Computer

Adobe Illustrator or other vector graphics software application

CREATE TESSELLATIONS TO DECORATE T-SHIRTS AND OTHER FABRICS

Time: **2–3 Hours**   Complexity: **Easy**

1. CONTEMPLATE SHAPES

Triangles, squares, and hexagons are the only regular geometric shapes that fit perfectly with themselves to cover a surface without leaving any gaps (I am using the word "regular" in a mathematical sense, to mean a shape that has all equal sides and equal angles).

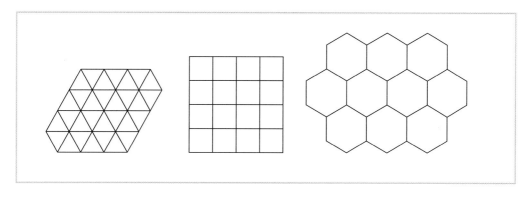

To make things more interesting, we can use a mix of these regular shapes. If we color them selectively. we can make them eye-catching. If we go further and introduce irregular shapes, the pattern loses some of its purity but can become more interesting and complex.

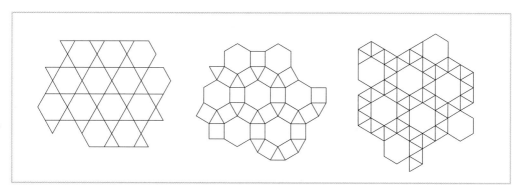

Illustrations by Charles Platt

2. CONSIDER SOFTWARE

The most obvious tessellation application is on fabric, using stencils or block printing. In one sense, this is very easy because you only have to make a few blocks or stencils, which you use repeatedly to create your pattern. The not-so-easy part is drawing and cutting the shapes precisely and assembling them accurately. Fortunately, computers are precise by nature. Graphics software has eased the process of creating tessellations, especially when you want to experiment quickly with different coloring schemes. You'll need software that creates images using vector graphics, meaning that instead of working with pixels (as in Photoshop), you are using mathematically precise points and lines. Adobe Illustrator is the best-known application that works in this way, with CorelDraw a close second. Personally, I use Illustrator 8, which sells for less than $30 on eBay. Even version 4 would be sufficient for pattern design.

3. PLAN YOUR PATTERN

First, we need to set up a library of basic polygons that all have the same edge lengths so that they will fit together.

NOTE: More recent versions of Illustrator include a tool that automatically creates polygons with any number of sides, but it does not allow you to control the edge lengths precisely. It's best to use the system described here.

3a. Decide how many sides your shape will have, and divide this number into 360. Suppose you want to draw a hexagon, which has 6 sides. You divide 360 by 6 and get 60. This is the "rotation angle," telling you how much you would turn if you were walking along the perimeter of a hexagon, reached a corner, and reoriented yourself to proceed along the next side.

3b. Now write a list of angles, beginning with your rotation angle, then doubling it, tripling it, and so on, till you get to 360. For a hexagon, the numbers look like this: 60, 120, 180, 240, 300, 360. This is as mathematical as we'll need to be.

4. CREATE YOUR SHAPE

4a. Using Illustrator, select the pen tool and click once in the center of the page to create a single point. With the point still selected, open the Move dialog box. Ignore the fields where you would enter horizontal and vertical values. In the Distance field, enter 1 inch, and in the Angle field, enter the first number on your list of angles (60 for a hexagon).

4b. Click Copy to create a second point. If your first point seems to disappear, go to the View menu and check the Artwork option.

4c. Now go back to the Move box, but this time enter the next angle number in your list, which will be 120 for a hexagon. Repeat until you have the necessary number of points to mark the corners of the shape.

4d. Using the Direct Selection tool (white arrow), select pairs of points, and use the Join command to create lines connecting them. You can use this system to create polygons with any number of sides. Now for the interesting part: fitting everything together.

5. FIT EVERYTHING TOGETHER

5a. To locate shapes accurately with Adobe Illustrator, you must use the Object Selection tool (black arrow) to drag an object by a corner point and snap it into place against another corner point. This is the only way to do precise work.

5b. If you use the Rotate tool to make shapes fit together, enter the exact number of degrees. Triangles, squares, and hexagons have a natural affinity for each other, while pentagons, heptagons, nonagons, and decagons are not so mutually compatible (those are polygons with 5, 7, 9, and 10 sides). You can still create tile patterns with the uncooperative shapes, but only if you don't mind introducing some irregular shapes between them. If you prefer to use physical objects, print as many copies as you need, cut them out, and start shuffling them around.

Adding color helps.

This pattern uses regular dodecagons (12-sided polygons) with triangles, squares, and hexagons around them.

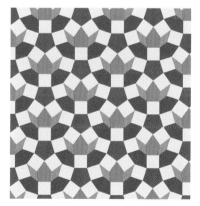

Regular shapes that don't fit together, such as pentagons, require irregular shapes to fill the gaps. To make this pattern, first draw a pentagon, then attach squares that are rotated by increments of 72 degrees. Make copies and place them corner-to-corner. Then draw the extra pieces (green, orange, and purple in this example), dragging their points so they align precisely by clicking into place with the corners of the squares.

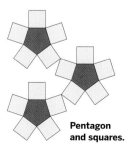

Pentagon and squares.

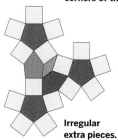

Irregular extra pieces.

6. CREATE TESSELLATIONS WITH YOUR OWN SKETCHES

If you want a break from geometry, you can create a free-form tessellation (go to craftzine.com/04/ tessellations for more examples.). Escher often depicted birds, probably because their cross-shaped silhouettes fit together easily in a tessellation.

Fish are also ideal candidates — and Escher used them too. The nose of a fish can fit into the tail of the same fish outline in front of it, while its body contains a mix of convex and concave curves that can also fit together. Look online (URL above) for simple sketches that I made to test this possibility.

6a. Begin with some quick sketches, and when you have a shape that seems promising, draw it with your illustration software so that you can make precise duplicates easily. Copy and paste it over a grid to see if it could work.

6b. If it still looks promising, fit the curves to a grid, aligning the anchor points (circled in blue) in your curves with the intersections in your grid. Use as few anchor points as possible. Some kind of grid underlies all repeating tessellations, but there's no rule that it must consist of squares. You can distort the grid, dragging the artwork with it to make the shapes more pleasing. Just remember that if you move one point, you have to move all the other points that will repeat with it. Because each fish spreads across 2 squares, and because the shape below is offset by a distance of 1 square, the grid points that must move together are diagonally opposite each other. I have labeled them A and B in the next step.

6c. If you work with Adobe Illustrator, use the Direct Selection tool and stretch a marquee over each "A" point in turn, holding down Shift to add to your selected points. The marquee will select the anchor points in the curves you have drawn, as well as the grid points beneath. When you stretch the grid, you also stretch your drawing, and everything will still automatically fit together. Keep fooling around with it until your pattern works!

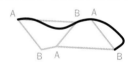

6d. Outline and fill with color and other details. Copy and paste as needed.

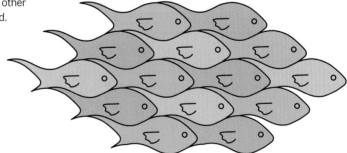

This technique is so much faster than working with pencil and paper that M.C. Escher would have been able to create 2 or 3 times as many tessellations if he had computer software to assist him in the construction process. Of course the fine execution of his prints give them their unique beauty, but as craftspeople, we can at least move a little closer to emulating his genius with the aid of technology. In fact, we may achieve results that used to be considered so difficult that few people have ever attempted to create this kind of art.

7. MARK YOUR PATTERN ON FABRIC

7a. Scale your shapes to the size you want, then print and tape together enough of them to extend from one edge of the cloth to the other.

7b. Use a long straightedge to make sure that all the shapes are aligned, then mark through the corner points to the fabric using a dressmaker's pencil. Move your entire pattern along, and repeat the process. The bigger your pattern is, the less you'll have to worry about cumulative errors. If your pattern is a free-form tesselation, carefully draw it using a cutout shape, or freehand as shown here, taking care to align it with your anchor points.

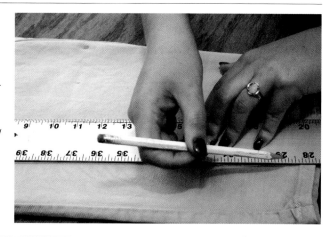

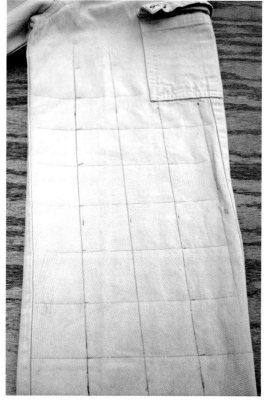

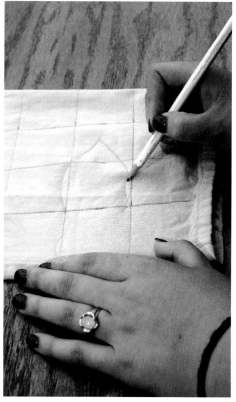

8. APPLY COLOR

You can use stencils, block printing, or paint freehand. Stencils are easier, especially if your computer printer will accept the thin sheets of plastic sold in stationery stores to make overhead transparencies.

8a. Print one shape onto each sheet of plastic, cut it out with an X-Acto knife, then align your plastic stencil with the marks on the fabric.

8b. Regular household spray paint works well with stencils on fabric, especially on white T-shirt cotton. The paint embeds itself in the weave and is colorfast. Use double-sided tape around the holes in your stencils, to prevent spray paint from getting underneath or blowing them away. You may also need to keep a rag handy, soaked in mineral spirits, to wipe the stencil from time to time.

NOTE: Check to make sure that the solvent won't dissolve the plastic, and always work in a well-ventilated area, using gloves, since solvents and spray paints are potential health hazards.

8c. To paint freehand without a stencil, use fabric paints as shown here.

8d. If you prefer block printing, you can cut your shapes out of wood, or make linocuts (*see "101: Linocuts" in Volume 02, page 134*). Block printing is the most potentially creative because it allows you to add ornamentation inside each shape. This also moves you toward the challenge of morphing the shape boundaries to make interlocking silhouettes of living things, as M.C. Escher did with such unique skill.

FINISH

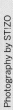

Photography by ST!ZO

Aerosol Artistry

Fine-tune your can control by watching the masters at work. BY ST!ZO WITH REVISE CMW AND OMENS

The beginnings of modern graffiti can be traced back to the late 60s when graffiti artists like TAKI 183 and Julio 204 used magic marker and spray paint to tag their names in the boroughs of New York City. By the mid-70s, graffiti artists moved to subway cars, painting them from top to bottom. Some people looked at it as vandalism and a sign of urban decay, but as time passed, graffiti became accepted by many as a true art form.

Today, many business owners ask graffiti writers to use their buildings as canvases for their imaginations. REVISE CMW and OMENS let me document their collaboration on a recent wall project, on the West Side of Chicago. Following is an explanation of the process they go through to create their pieces.

+ TAG IT: **GRAFFITI**

A   B

Fig. A: REVISE CMW plots out his design with his first outline. It's important to use an outline color that will blend easily with the main colors of the piece.

Fig. B: OMENS works on the fill, the second step in the process. To save time, fat caps are used to increase coverage.

Materials

- » **Paint mask** to protect those lungs!
- » **Latex gloves** to reduce cleanup time
- » **Paint tray and roller**
- » **Cover-up paint** any kind, several gallons, depending on the size of the wall
- » **Spray paint** in your choice of colors
- » **Extra caps** in case of clogging
- » **Creativity**

Though it's nearly impossible to describe how to make each and every letter in this piece, watching the process gives a window into how amazing works like this are created. Of course, not every graffiti writer uses the method explained here. Graffiti is a free-form art and there are no rules in the way of its application.

Before you start, make sure you acquire a "legal wall" to apply your artwork to. "The hardest thing to do is to get your first legal wall," says OMENS. "Owners of buildings will ask you to place your art on their building if they're familiar with your skills and reputation."

Once a graffiti writer earns the respect of the community, other walls and painting opportunities will be offered. REVISE CMW adds, "Doing a wall is not just painting — it's a production. A lot of preparation goes into the whole process."

1. Cover the wall with paint.

Using your roller, tray, and cover-up paint, coat the existing wall to create a blank canvas for your piece. Section off the wall so that you have enough room to create your masterpiece, making sure it's visible to passersby.

Fig. C: REVISE CMW carves out his design with the second outline. Fig. D: REVISE CMW and OMENS do fills and background together to save time.

Fig. E: OMENS adds background embellishments.

2. Form the initial outline.

The initial outline is a quick sketch to map out the area and shapes you'll be working with (Figure A). Make sure you use a color that can easily blend in with the colors in the next step of the process, the fill. The sketch doesn't have to be exact or detailed at this point; spray paint is a forgiving medium to work with.

3. Fill.

Once the initial outline is created, fill in the area with the colors you've selected (Figure B). To save time, fat caps are used for more paint coverage. Fat caps output more paint than the standard caps provided with cans of paint. (For a quick guide to caps, check out craftzine.com/go/spraypaint.)

4. Add the secondary outline.

While the tail end of the fill is drying, you can start the second outline (Figure C). This outline will define the shapes and lines you created in the initial outline. A nice contrasting color can be selected to really make your design stand out.

5. Add shadows and 3D blocks.

To add depth to your design, you can add shadowing and 3D blocks to the secondary outline.

6. Add background images and embellishments.

If your theme requires the use of background images, you might want to add them now rather than at the end. Background images are usually subtle embellishments that don't overtake the main image (Figures E and G). Characters can also be added at this point (Figure F).

Characters sometimes serve to unify collaborations such as this one. Because the styles of the artists are so different, the choice of colors, characters, and background elements are ways of unifying the two sides of the piece.

7. Clean it up.

This is called cutting. Cutting is a way to achieve sharp lines and mask over your mess-ups. Take your fill color and spray over your outlines to cut off the lines you don't want, sort of like an eraser.

Fig. F: Characters are added to give the artwork a little more pizzazz, or to unify collaborations.
Fig. G: REVISE CMW adds the aura to his piece.

Fig. H: REVISE CMW and OMENS put their signature tags on the wall to let people know who created this piece (for CRAFT!). Fig. I: Both artists finish up the wall.

8. Finish with the aura.

When your piece is cleaned up and completed, an aura is applied (Figure G). This is a final outline around the body of your piece. The color usually contrasts with the second outline and the background. The aura separates your artwork from the background details and gives it extra emphasis.

9. Sign it.

Now your masterpiece is complete (Figure H). You want people to know who created the artwork, and you want to represent the crew that you're a part of. This is called a tag. At this time, you can add any other messages, taglines, or dedications to let viewers know why the piece was created.

Special thanks to REVISE CMW and OMENS for taking me out with them and helping me illustrate the ways of the urban artist. Chicago represent!

Since 1994, ST!ZO has been utilizing his talents to do good deeds in the Chicago hip-hop scene. His heavy involvement with the community has had a big influence on his music and artistic endeavors. Check out his creations at gurelea.com and myspace.com/djstizo.

Knit Caution Tape

Police line: do not cross-stitch.

BY MICHELLE KEMPNER

Photograph by Steve Lambert

I n the days before mass production, things had to be made by hand. From stockings to gloves, knitters worked long hours making beautiful garments and accessories. Who's to say that the earliest cops didn't knit their own police tape?

I first knitted police tape in 2006 as an experiment. I wanted to learn how to knit with color, incorporate text into my craft projects, and design something that my partners at the Graffiti Research Lab might find useful for urban pranks and hijinks. The result is a simple pattern for knitted police tape that's perfect for crafty barricades, marking a crime scene, or wearing as a unique urban-inspired scarf. Experiment with your own color-switching technique and customize your version for the protestors without permits in your town.

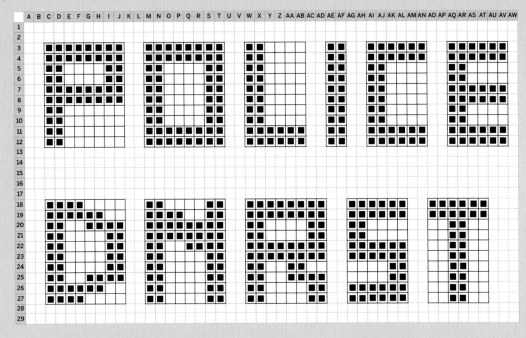

Materials

- » **Worsted-weight acrylic yarn,**
  2 skeins gold and 1 skein black
  I used Dark Horse Fantasy #26
  and #1, but you can swap these
  for your own faves.
- » **US 8 knitting needles**
- » **Tapestry needle**

This pattern includes a letter chart and 2 variations
of the tape: one that knits fast for rapid production
and one that takes more time for a polished look.

Pattern 1 (for rapid production)

1. Cast on 18 stitches in the gold color.
2. Knit 2, purl 2 to end. On wrong side, purl 2, knit 2
to end. Continue in 2×2 rib pattern.
3. After 16 rows, begin knitting the text according
to the letter chart. To work the letters, knit 2, purl 2,
and then begin working each letter as shown.
4. Once the police tape has reached the desired
length, bind off and sew in all ends. Block for good
measure. One skein of yarn creates about 9 feet
of police tape.

Pattern 2 (more finished look)

1. Cast on 29 stitches in gold.
2. Knit 14, purl 1, knit 14. Continue in stockinette

with the 15th stitch always purl on the right side and
knit on the wrong side.
3. After 16 rows, begin knitting the text on an RS
row according to the letter chart. This is a 2-sided
pattern with the letters appearing on only one side.
Therefore, knit 2 stitches before working the letter.
After the letter, complete the row in pattern.
4. Once the police tape has reached the desired
length, bind off. Sew in all ends. Block the police tape.
5. To finish, put the right sides together and use a
tapestry needle to seam the open side using a back-
stitch. Pull the police tape right side out, and you're
done. One skein of yarn creates more than 4 feet
of police tape.

Letter chart

Each letter is separated by 2 rows of gold; each
word is separated by 6 rows of gold; and each group
of words is separated by 16 rows of gold. One group
of words is about 3 feet long.

➕ For other variations on knitted police tape,
check out *Crime of Fashion* by Marnie MacLean
on magknits.com.

➕ For more knitting projects in the urban landscape, visit knittaplease.com.

Michelle Kempner has a degree from NYU's Interactive
Telecommunications Program. She lives in New York and
splits her time between technology and crafts.

Moss Graffiti

Try this alternative to spray paint, and leave your mark in the way of gardeners past.

BY HELEN NODDING

Photography by Helen Nodding

The possibility of growing moss graffiti occurred to me during one of those dull days at work when your thoughts wander. A quick internet search showed me that I wasn't the first person to ask the question, "How does moss grow?" In fact, many genius gardeners had even come up with a recipe for a moss milkshake! Next I wondered if you could use this recipe to grow your own designs and create a kind of moss graffiti, and it would appear that you can.

The Moss Graffiti recipe was previously published in *Interlude Magazine*, Issue 2, and *Craftivity*, edited by Tsia Carson, Harper Collins, 2006.

A

B

C

Fig. A: Gathered moss. Fig. B: Rinsing mud off the clumps. The process of growing moss is very much dependent on selecting exactly the right location in the right weather conditions. If your climate is too dry, grow the moss indoors and transplant it outside once your pattern has successfully grown (Fig. C). It took approximately 6 weeks for this design to be ready.

Materials

» **Several clumps of garden moss**
» **1 can of beer, or pot of natural yogurt, or 12oz buttermilk** See which works best for your location.
» **½tsp sugar**
» **Blender**
» **Plastic container with a lid**
» **Paintbrush and spray mister**

NOTE: For indoor growing, you'll also need compost and a seed tray.

1. Gather moss.

First gather together several clumps of moss. You can find moss growing between the cracks in paving stones, near leaky drains, on trees ... basically, moss loves damp and shady places. Mosses do not have roots but use rhizoids to attach themselves to surfaces, meaning that you can easily collect moss by hand or with a spatula. Clean off as much of the mud as possible by soaking it in water.

2. Make the moss milkshake.

Put the moss in a blender and add beer (or yogurt or buttermilk) and sugar. Blend just long enough to create a smooth, creamy consistency, like a thick milkshake. Pour the mixture into a plastic container.

3. Create your design.

Find a suitable location onto which you can apply your moss milkshake (a good indicator is somewhere that moss is already growing). Paint on your chosen design (either freehand or using a stencil).

4. Tend your graffiti.

If possible, try to water your masterpiece daily with a spray mister. Soon the bits of blended moss should begin to recuperate, maintaining your design before eventually colonizing the whole area.

➕ Learn about mosses at craftzine.com/go/moss.

Helen Nodding is an artist who lives and works in London. As well as her own work (storiesfromspace.co.uk), she often collaborates with the London-based group Spacehijackers, who explore and critique the use of public space.

Order now to become a Craft subscriber!

craftzine.com/subscribe

Craft:
transforming traditional crafts™

Subscribe now to receive a full year of CRAFT (four quarterly issues) for just $34.95!* You'll **save over 40%** off the newsstand price.

Name

Address

City   State

Zip/Postal Code   Country

Email Address

*$34.95 includes US delivery. Please add $5 for Canada and $15 for all other countries.

B7CTB

craftzine.com

Craft:
transforming traditional crafts™

Subscribe now to receive a full year of CRAFT (four quarterly issues) for just $34.95!* You'll **save over 40%** off the newsstand price.

Name

Address

City   State

Zip/Postal Code   Country

Email Address

*$34.95 includes US delivery. Please add $5 for Canada and $15 for all other countries.

B7CBB

Order now to become a Craft subscriber!

craftzine.com/subscribe

NO POSTAGE
NECESSARY
IF MAILED
IN THE
UNITED STATES

BUSINESS REPLY MAIL

FIRST-CLASS MAIL   PERMIT NO 865   NORTH HOLLYWOOD CA

POSTAGE WILL BE PAID BY ADDRESSEE

Craft:

PO BOX 17046
NORTH HOLLYWOOD CA 91615-9588

NO POSTAGE
NECESSARY
IF MAILED
IN THE
UNITED STATES

BUSINESS REPLY MAIL

FIRST-CLASS MAIL   PERMIT NO 865   NORTH HOLLYWOOD CA

POSTAGE WILL BE PAID BY ADDRESSEE

Craft:

PO BOX 17046
NORTH HOLLYWOOD CA 91615-9588

Photography by Dora Reneé Wilkerson

Hay Twine Rug

Loom-knit a durable outdoor rug with plastic yarn. BY DORA RENEÉ WILKERSON

Most anyone who has livestock will have twine from their hay or straw bales. This twine — commonly called hay or baler twine — usually gets thrown out or burned. Instead of tossing it, why not make a hay twine rug?

Hay twine that's made of plastic can be used to make wonderful outdoor rugs. And you don't have to own livestock to get this plastic "yarn." If you're not close to a Tractor Supply Co. or meat-packing supply store, you can purchase it online at a packing supply outlet such as packandseal.com.

A loom-knit twine rug grabs dirt right off the bottom of your shoes. The dirt falls between the knits and under the rug. When the rug gets dirty, you just hose it off. You'll feel good about your rug because it's functional and great for the environment.

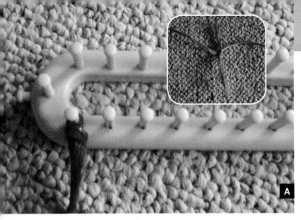

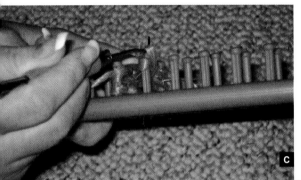

Fig. A: Connecting the twine and attaching it to the loom. Fig. B: You'll be wrapping all your pegs on your loom just like this, in a figure 8 stitch two times. Fig. C: How to bind off with a crochet hook.

Fig. D: Twine rug close-up. The rug on page 113 is kept outside and used a lot. Even though it's over 2 years old, all the knits are still together. Inset shows top row placed on top of bottom row.

Materials

» **Hay twine, also called baler twine or polypropylene twine** The plastic type of twine is preferred, usually orange in color. Rope-type twine is harder to work with.
» **Tapestry needle**
» **Hook tool**
» **Crochet hook**
» **Board loom, 18" or longer** I used a Knifty Knitter long loom.

1. Connect the twine.

Tie the pieces of twine into one long strand. Simply knot them together at the ends — if you tie the knots tight enough, they help clean your shoes better! You do this a little at a time. Connect maybe 4 or 5 pieces, and knit. Then go back to attaching more (just so you don't have a big mess in the house).

2. Knit onto your loom.

Knit in a figure 8 stitch from the first peg to the last peg on your loom. Knit 1 over 1 and knit off. Repeat until you reach the length you would like. This rug was done in 90 rows, and measures 14"×30". (If you want a wider rug, use the Knifty Knitter 22" Blue loom. If you want a longer rug, just keep knitting more rows.)

3. Remove the rug from your loom.

Place the entire top row onto the bottom row like the picture shown here (inset, Figure D).

To bind off, crochet each peg, one at a time, off the loom. After the last peg, tie a square knot at the last bind off stitch.

My rug is kept outside and is used tons. It's over 2 years old and all the knits are still together. The only visible wear is the color, which has been bleached out over time.

Dora Reneé Wilkerson lives in Marion, Ohio, with her husband, two children, three horses, and two dairy goats. She has multiple hobbies and keeps two blogs: bricoreandfamily. blogspot.com and amishrugsandmore.blogspot.com.

Beach Ball Bench

Upholster and assemble a modern vinyl seat.

BY MATT MARANIAN

Although this bench isn't actually made from beach balls, it is evocative of the classic summer standard. Add a dash of modernism and a pinch of bowling alley utilitarianism, and you've got a sturdy piece of upholstered furniture for less effort than you'd expend rolling 3 frames.

If you find upholstery daunting, rest assured that there is no tuft-and-fold trickery here; if you can passably wrap a birthday gift, consider yourself pre-qualified. As far as assembly goes, a staple gun and a drill are about as complicated as things are gonna get.

Foam rubber can be had at many fabric or futon stores, and the pipe legs and flanges can be purchased, cut-to-size, at any hardware store worth its weight in cheap goods.

Photography by Matt Maranian

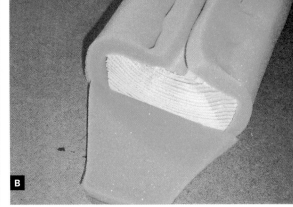

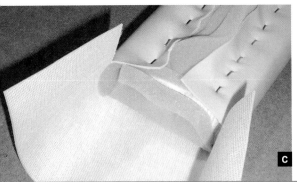
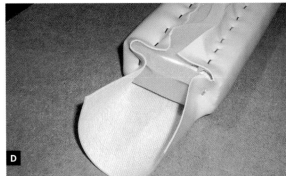

Fig. A: Trimming the foam rubber for a tight upholstered edge.
Fig. B: Taper the ends.

Fig. C: Take care not to overcut the top edge.
Fig. D: Pull ends taut to keep a clean upholstered edge.

Materials

» **2×4 studs*** cut to four 48" lengths
» **½" sheet foam rubber** enough to cut into four 10"×60" pieces, with extra trim
» **Staple gun**
» **Box of staples** I used T20 ⅜"×10mm staples.
» **Scissors**
» **54"-wide vinyl upholstery fabric** 1½ yards
» **1½" drywall screws (16)**
» **#10×1" wood screws (16)**
» **½" plywood 14"×36" piece**
» **Drill**
» **5/32" drill bit**
» **¾"×18" galvanized threaded plumbing pipe (4)**
» **¾" floor flanges (4)**
» **Phillips screw bit**
» **1" rubber furniture leg caps (4)**

* Note from the Materials List:
If you've never worked with 2×4 studs before, it may be surprising — even disconcerting — for you to discover that a 2×4 actually measures more like 1½"×3½". Don't be concerned, that's just the way life is sometimes.

1. Pad the bench slats.

Cut the foam rubber sheets into 4 pieces measuring 10"×60". Once cut, center a 48" 2×4 over one of your 10"x60" foam pieces.

Starting from the center, gently pull the edge of the foam rubber taut over the side of the 2×4 (being careful not to tear the foam), and staple into place. Space staples approximately 1" apart, all the way to each end, finishing both sides. Repeat with the remaining three 2×4s and foam rubber pieces.

Trim the foam rubber flush to each end along the top 3 edges of the 2×4, so that the end trims lie flat (Figure A). Cut the sides of each end piece at inverted angles so that the end pieces taper slightly (Figure B). Fold each end piece over the end of the 2×4, staple into place, and trim the overhanging foam. Repeat with the remaining 3 slats.

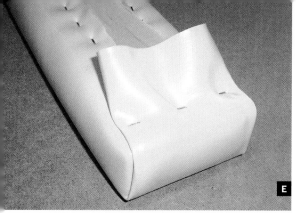

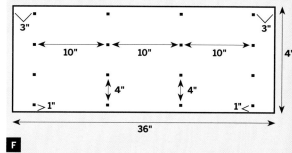

E F

G H

Fig. E: Staple vinyl into place and trim excess.
Fig. F: Drill 16 lead holes through the plywood base, spaced as shown, for attaching the bench slats.

Fig. G: Secure each upholstered slat to the plywood base.
Fig. H: Secure the flanges wherever you like for leg placement.

2. Upholster the bench slats.

Cut the vinyl into 12"-wide sections. Lay a piece of vinyl, backside up, on a work surface. Center a padded 2×4 slat on top. Fold and staple the vinyl upholstery, just as you did the foam rubber (leaving the ends untouched at this point). Repeat with the remaining 3 slats.

Now open up the vinyl end trim by cutting away the top sides, just about ¼" shy from each outside corner of the 2×4 (Figure C). Make inverted angle cuts on each side of the vinyl end trim. Pull and fold the side edges of the vinyl upholstery around the sides of the padded 2×4, and staple into place (Figure D).

Using the foam rubber trim, cut eight 1"×3" pieces. Tuck a piece into the open end of the stapled vinyl. To finish the upholstery with straight-tucked edges, pinch the sides of the end trim, and pull and fold over the end of the 2×4. Then staple into place (Figure E). Trim excess vinyl, and staple down any puckering. Repeat with the other 7 ends.

3. Assemble the seat.

With a ⁵⁄₃₂" drill bit, drill lead holes through the plywood as per Figure F. Place the upholstered bench

slats face down and flush against one another, with their ends lined up straight and square.

Center the plywood sheet 1" from the front and back edges of the assembled slat area, and 3" from each end. Using the drywall screws, secure the plywood base to the bench slats — the plywood ends up underneath the slats, of course (Figure G).

4. Give it some legs.

Position the pipe flanges 2" from the front and rear edges of the upholstered bench seat, and 3" from each end. Secure into place using the wood screws (Figure H). Attach the pipe to the flanges, and finish the pipe ends with 1" rubber leg caps.

Flip it and sit ... or just stand back and admire your work.

Matt Maranian is a best-selling writer, designer, and bon vivant whose books include *PAD* and *PAD Parties*. He lives in New England.

Get a Rise Out of Sourdough

The yeasty way to a truly good loaf. BY ERIC SMILLIE

My heart sank as I stared at the dark, deflated crust, hardly the loaf I had hoped to bake using wild yeast from a home-fermented starter. I needed help. I found clarity in Laura McNall, a baker for 22 years with the Cheese Board Collective, a worker-owned cheese shop and bakery in Berkeley, Calif., that uses more than a dozen 14-pound buckets of sourdough starter every day. "When you're dealing with fermentation," consoles McNall, "it's alive and it's got a life of its own ... Sometimes it doesn't work out." Eventually, however, it did. Now my only problem is keeping my tangy sourdough loaves out of the hands of my ravenous roommates.

Photography by Eric Smillie

Fig. A: The starter equipment and flour/water mixture.
Fig. B: A close-up of the starter after a few days of
feeding; note the foam and bubbles.

Fig. C: The starter and other ingredients in a mixing
bowl. Fig. D: The mixed dough.

Materials

For the starter:
» Flour
» Filtered, non-chlorinated water

For the bread:
» **Active starter** (within half a day
   of climax)**, about 2 cups**
» **Unbleached white flour, 3 cups**
» **2tsp kosher salt**
» **Water, up to ½ cup**

The magic of sourdough is that you can leaven
bread with a culture of yeast and lactobacillus (the
same bacteria that turn milk into cheese) drawn
from thin air, just by mixing flour and water in a glass
jar. The yeast creates gluten and makes the dough
rise, while the bacteria produce acid that imparts a
distinct flavor and keeps spoiling microbes at bay.

Every place has its own airborne microorganism
population, and each can give rise to a starter with
a unique character, says sourdough sage Ed Wood,

the author of *Classic Sourdoughs: A Home Baker's
Handbook*. Wood has been baking for some 50
years and sells heirloom starters from places like
South Africa and Italy through Sourdoughs International (sourdo.com). Contrary to popular belief, he
says, a starter can travel. Some people think "that if
you send a culture somewhere else in the world, it will
be contaminated by the local flora and fauna," he says.
"That, basically, is a lot of baloney."

Once established, a healthy starter can last
forever. Wood claims he collected a starter in Giza,
Egypt, that hadn't changed much since about 2500
BC. The oldest sourdough cultures are in the Middle
East, and, he adds, "by and large, were passed from
father to son for hundreds of years." Here's how to
start an heirloom of your very own.

1. Start the starter.

Thoroughly mix ½ cup flour with ⅓ cup water in a
mason jar. Cover with a towel or loose lid, and let it sit
in a warm place for a day. Stir occasionally to aerate.

2. Enrich the base.

After 24 hours, pour out all but about ¼ of the mixture,
and thoroughly mix in 1 cup flour and ¾ cup water.

Fig. E: The kneaded dough. My batches always seem to need about a ½ cup of water to get to the right consistency. Fig. F: A close-up of thegluten window; this effect will tell you when it's the right consistency.

Fig. G: The covered dough rising. Fig. H: The baked sourdough loaf, ready to eat! You should hear a hollow sound when you knock on a finished loaf.

3. Keep feeding the starter.

Repeat Step 2 daily. In 3 to 5 days, the starter should have a rich, beery smell and be bubbly throughout, climaxing in frothy activity some hours after each feeding. A day before baking, feed it enough to meet your recipe with some left over.

Different instructions recommend bafflingly different ratios of flour to water. The wetter the starter, the more quickly it will run through its life cycle. My starters do best at banana-milkshake consistency, but cultures and environments differ, so experiment with ratios and temperatures as necessary. Wood suggests that bakers put new starters outside, where wild yeast will be prevalent.

4. Knead the dough.

Thoroughly mix the starter, flour, and salt, and let the dough rest for 10 minutes. Then knead the dough gently but persistently for about 15 minutes, until you can make a gluten window — a thin, translucent membrane of dough that forms when you slowly stretch a walnut-sized lump between your thumb and forefinger. Add flour or water, by the tablespoon, to moisten or dry the dough as needed.

5. Let it sit. Then sit some more.

Shape the dough into a ball, put it in a large bowl, cover with a damp towel, and let it rise in a warm spot until it doubles in size, about 5 hours. Then gently press the air out of the dough, form it into a loaf, and place it on an oiled baking pan under a moist towel until it doubles in size, about 2 more hours.

6. Bake.

Set the oven rack to medium height, and preheat to 400° about 15 minutes before baking. Mist the dough lightly with water, slide it into the oven, and bake for 30 to 40 minutes. Cool on a wire rack.

When baking, always save a bit of starter from which to regenerate. To preserve, let it sit for a few hours after feeding, then cover it loosely and put it in the fridge, where Wood says it can stay for as long as 6 months without new food. When you're ready to bake again, feed it the night before, and by morning your wild pet will be back in action.

Eric Smillie is a freelance journalist and fermented-food devotee.

Extracting Squid Ink

Get your tentacles on ink that can be used for printing or cooking. BY CHRISTY CANIDA

Photography by Noah Weinstein

Squid are wonderful creatures. They're available in sizes small to giant, taste great, and are a fabulous source of natural ink. Squid use the ink to confuse predators, but you can use it for cooking or printing. Learn how to harvest your own fresh squid ink, so when you're stranded on a desert island, you'll have the best SOS messages around!

To get started, catch or buy your squid. If you buy, make sure they are still whole; if they're pre-cleaned, all of that wonderful ink will be gone. If the flesh has started to turn pink (instead of cream or white) or smell, buy your squid elsewhere. Boxes of frozen squid should be solid, without evidence of leakage or thawing. Small squid are tastier and easier to cook, but they have less ink. If you're going to be printing, get lots of the little guys.

HARVEST IT: SQUID INK

A B

C D

Fig. A: The full squid; pull the head and tentacles out of the body cavity to get at the ink. Fig. B: Look for the silvery sac attached to the guts. Slide the knife underneath it and cut out from the center to remove it.

Fig. C: The ink sac once it's been detached from the squid's body. Fig. D: To get at the secondary ink sacs behind the eyes, remove the beak by squeezing the head to expose it and then pinching it off.

Materials

» Squid (1 or more)
» Nonporous bowl
» Knife
» Strainer
» Silicone spatula

For printing:
» Ink-carrier medium
» Printing tools
» Paper

For cooking:
(recipe online)
» Olive oil
» Onion
» Garlic
» ½ cup white wine
» 1 cup short grain rice
» 2–6 cups stock
» Parsley
» Seasoning

1. Extract the ink.

You will be extracting squid ink from 2 sources: the main ink sac in the body and small, secondary deposits behind the eyes. First, pull the head and tentacles out of the body cavity. The guts will come along with the head; look for the small, thin, silvery sac about halfway along. Carefully detach the ink sac, taking care not to puncture it. It's attached at the ends, so just slip your knife underneath and cut away from the center to remove it.

2. Choose your own adventure.

Now is the choice point: what do you want to do with your ink? If you want to print with the ink, go to Step 3. If you want to cook with the ink, go to Step 4.

3. Print with squid ink.

If you plan to print with your ink, put a tablespoon of matte medium, linseed oil, or other ink carrier medium into a small nonporous glass, ceramic, or metal bowl (squid ink can stain plastic, unglazed ceramic, and cloth). Keep in mind that it's easy to dilute your ink later; leave it concentrated now to keep your options open.

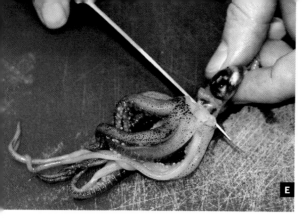

E F

G H

Fig. E: Cut the tentacles off below the eyes, taking care not to puncture the eyes. Fig. F: The dark spots behind the squid's retina are the secondary ink sacs.

Fig. G: Poke your knife into the ink sacs and squeeze out the remaining drops of ink into your bowl. Fig. H: Squid ink risotto topped with pan-fried squid.

A. Puncture the sacs.

If the ink sacs are large, gently puncture them with your knife, and squeeze the contents into the bowl. If the ink sacs are small, or you'd like to avoid getting your hands any messier and potentially squirting the wall with squid ink, simply drop the entire ink sac into the bowl and puncture it with the tip of your knife. We'll strain the sacs out later. Squeeze behind the head to extrude the beak, and remove it from the center of the tentacles. Now cut the tentacles off just below the eyes, taking care not to puncture the eyes. From the cut end you can see the ink deposits: they're the dark bits just behind the silvery backside of the squid's retina. Poke your knife into the ink, and gently squeeze the additional drops into the bowl. Repeat the process with the rest of your squid, setting aside the tentacles and bodies for dinner.

B. Strain and use the ink.

Strain your ink into another non-reactive container, and squeeze any remaining ink sacs against the mesh with the back of a non-staining silicone spatula, to make sure they're thoroughly empty.

Rinse the bowl and strainer with more of your ink carrier medium, and scrape both with the spatula to remove any last bits of ink. Discard the ink sacs, and

stir your ink into the carrier medium. Test for color and dilute as necessary, then print as you would with normal ink. (*See CRAFT, Volume 02, page 134, "101: Linocuts" for a linoleum block printing tutorial.*)

Be sure to use the ink immediately, or refrigerate it for use soon — just like squid, the ink will start to smell if you leave it out! Wash your printing tools with extra care as well.

4. Cook with squid ink.

If you plan to cook with your ink, put a tablespoon of water or vinegar into a nonporous bowl. As in Step 3, deposit the ink sacs directly into the bowl and puncture them with the tip of a knife.

A classic way to show off your hard-won squid ink is to give color to pasta or rice. Go to craftzine.com/04/harvest_squid for an easy recipe for squid ink risotto with squid (pictured above). Or, make your favorite risotto, and process the squid while the risotto cooks. When the risotto is almost done, add your squid ink.

Christy Canida is an MIT-trained biologist who loves cutting things up, experimenting with food, and dancing in costumes. She's the community and marketing manager for instructables.com.

Risotto photograph by Jess Liotta

Candles from Scratch

Gather old cans, containers, and half-used candles to make brilliant, new light. BY LEAH PETERSON

Y ou don't need expensive equipment to make your own candles at home. You can use a variety of containers with smooth sides for molds, including thick plastic or metal measuring cups and muffin tins. An old pancake hot plate and cleaned food cans make a great double boiler. Just remember that whatever you use will most likely be covered in wax and not a good candidate for food use afterwards. Paraffin wax can be purchased at craft stores in large blocks, but you can also use old candle leftovers.

Materials

- » **Molds or reusable candle containers**
- » **Hot plate**
- » **Empty food cans** 16 ounces or larger
- » **Wick-centering sticks**
- » **Candle scents** (optional)
- » **Wax** new or used
- » **Measuring cup**
- » **Scissors**
- » **Dull knife**
- » **Heavy pliers or oven mitt**
- » **Long-handled spoon**
- » **Long-handled Phillips screwdriver**
- » **Small Phillips screwdriver**
- » **Mold screws**
- » **Mold sealer**
- » **Metal core wick and wick tabs**
- » **Wax dye**
- » **Hammer** (optional)

❋ TIPS

» Never pour used water down a sink drain after candle making — instead, discard the water on a dirt patch in the yard.

» Never leave melting wax unattended. Flash points for wax vary by type. Keep the temperature below 210°F to avoid a fire hazard.

» The water in the hot plate should never boil. If bubbles begin to form, turn the temperature down immediately by at least 5°, otherwise a can could overturn. When the water is the correct temperature, you should see a slight bit of steam and a few slow, small bubbles rising to the top.

» If you do accidentally spill hot wax on an uncovered surface, don't disturb it until it's cooled completely. Large sections of cold wax are much easier to clean up with a dull blade than warm wax that has been smeared thinly.

» You can coat the candle mold interior with a small amount of cooking spray. Use a paper towel to rub the inside, and make sure the coating is even and thin. Bubbles or puddles of spray will leave pockets in the wax.

» Reuse non-metal candle containers by putting them in the microwave for 15 seconds at a time. Use a blunt knife and a paper towel to wipe softened wax residue in between turns.

Before starting, cover every work surface with thick plastic — a few layers of trash bags will work.

1. Melt the wax.

Wash the metal food cans, one for each color. Break large pieces of wax into smaller chunks (to melt faster). Use a hammer if necessary. When recycling candles, remove old wicks and labels as completely as possible. Weigh the cans down with wax chips, then fill the hot plate with water, about ¾" from the top. Heat the water to 210°F.

2. Prepare the molds.

While the wax melts, get the molds ready. When choosing a wick, consider the diameter of the mold. Use thinner wicks for votives, and thicker wicks for larger molds. If the container is very wide, you can use a couple of wicks placed a few inches apart. Wicks with metal cores can be easier to work with since they are stiffer and straighter. Cut the wicks a few inches longer than the molds.

For votives or reusable containers, insert the wick into the metal wick tab, and crimp with pliers. Store-bought metal molds come with a small hole drilled into the bottom, where the wick will be pushed through. Use a small screw, available with candle supplies, to tighten and hold the wick on the outside. Use mold sealer to completely seal around the

screw and wick poking out of the end. This will be the finished candle's top.

3. Color your candles.

Add dye after all the wax chips have melted. You can make endless combinations with red, yellow, and blue. White is also helpful to soften a color and make it creamy-looking. If desired, add a few drops or chips of candle scent right before pouring.

4. Pour the wax.

Use pliers or oven mitts to hold the cans. When lifting the cans, do not drip water into the other cans of wax. You can also use a measuring cup to fill the molds. Fill the molds to about ¼" below the rim. Save some wax for topping off. After filling the molds, lower the hot plate to just under 200°F.

Deep or wide molds need a wick-centering stick. Use the stick to hold the wick in the center after pouring. Tying the wick around a pencil also works. Use metal-core wicks for votives and small molds. Wait 60–90 seconds after pouring, then use a long Phillips screwdriver to center the wick. Press down firmly to stick the wick to the slightly cooler wax on the bottom of the mold.

5. Top off the candles.

Smaller and thinner molds cool quickly. Wax will

Photography by Leah Peterson

A

B

C

D

Fig. A: Everything you'll need to make your candles.
Fig. B: Melting the wax. Separate colors, or your end
product will look muddy. Remove old wicks and labels
if possible. Fig. C: Pouring the wax into the mold.

Cut the wicks a few inches longer than the molds.
Then fill the molds to about ¼" from the rim.
Fig. D: Straightening the wicks. Use the stick to hold
the wick straight after pouring.

begin to seize and form a nipple around the wick.
When the outside of the mold is warm but not too
hot to hold, and the wax appears opaque, use your
reserve wax to top off the candles. Completely fill
the molds, allowing the new wax to crown slightly.
Cooler wax works best for topping off and should
give an even top when fully cooled.

6. Cool down.

Let thicker and taller molds cool overnight. Smaller
ones need only about 3 hours. When fully cooled,
put the molds directly into the freezer for 5 minutes.

7. Release the candles from their molds.

Turn votives on their sides and tap. They should slide
right out. For larger molds, take off the mold sealer,
remove the screw, and place the mold in the freezer
upside down. Candles should fall out on their own after a few minutes, or may require a few taps and gentle
tugs on the wick. Trim wicks to ½" before burning.

Did your candle not turn out as perfectly as you
had hoped? Smooth rough edges out on the bottom
of a warm hot plate. When the hot plate cools, use
a dull blade to remove the wax.

For Stripes: Let each color cool 1 hour before pouring the next color. Thicker stripes need longer. When
using a mold, don't let the layer completely cool, or
the next layer may not adhere properly.

For Sand Candles: Place wax-filled cans directly
in hot coals. While the wax melts, use paper cups
or sand toys to create votive shapes in moist sand.
Poke metal core wicks into the centers, about 1" into
the sand, and extending at least 1" over the tops of
the molds. Using pliers or oven mitts, carefully and
slowly pour melted wax into the molds, aiming for
the centers and trying not to disturb the sand along
the edges. Reserve some wax for topping off and
place the cans back in the coals. Let the candles
cool until tops are thick and opaque. Remove the
cans of wax from the coals until you see slight
thickening along the sides, then top off your sand
candles. Let them cool completely. Remove the
candles, trim the wicks, and brush off excess sand.

Leah Peterson is a crafter, writer, photographer, artist, mom,
and human. She reuses, restores, and recycles. You can find
her at leahpeah.com.

Pop Bottle Lamp

Shed some light with a vintage or unusual soda bottle. BY JASON TORCHINSKY AND SALLY MYERS

Photography by Sally Myers

I t's both a blessing and a curse, seeing value in crap. On the plus side, you can get all sorts of amazing things almost for free; on the minus, you can get all sorts of amazing things almost for free. Once you've trained your keen eye to look past prosaic notions of what's worthy, you'll end up swamped with amazing things you have no idea what to do with.

For my fiancée and myself, those amazing things were vintage and unusual soda bottles. They come in a dazzling variety of shapes and styles, and they often have wonderful silk-screened or printed graphics. The vintage ones can be found abundantly in rural and Southern antique stores (our families are both from the South), and the new ones even come with the bonus of 12 or so ounces of delicious soda.

Materials

- » **Glass soda bottle and lampshade**
- » **Candelabra-sized light bulb and bulb socket**
- » **110V 2-lead electrical cord** about 6–8 feet, no grounding wire needed, clear insulation preferred
- » **Electric drill**
- » **Glass/masonry drill bit** $5/16$" or so
- » **Wall-socket plug end**
- » **¾" PVC pipe adapter (slip x male threaded)** I used part number 436-007. The slip-fitting end goes over the bottle top; the male threaded end accepts the socket inside it, so the threads themselves aren't necessary. You might experiment with slightly different PVC pipe fittings.
- » **Gaffer's, duct, or electrical tape**
- » **In-line electrical switch**
- » **Styrofoam wine bottle shipper** (optional)

After amassing an ever-expanding collection of old bottles, I got the ultimatum to do something with the big, rattly collection or get rid of it. Sally's idea was to make them into lamps, and the more I thought about it, the more natural the idea seemed. Old, heavy soda bottles are pretty much a bulb and a couple of wires away from being a lamp, anyway, so why not give these old vessels some new life?

The trick here is to do as little to the bottle as possible. They make such great table lamp bodies as it is, you really just need to pick a shade. That, and do a bit of tricky glass drilling.

1. Pick a bottle.

This is the fun part. Ours is a world full of great soda bottles, once you start looking. The best ones are real vintage ones, as they are often nice and heavy, which will keep the lamp stable, and they usually have graphics printed right on the bottle, which are preferable to paper labels. Think about the colors of the bottle and the printing, and how they will match your lampshade. Check in thrift stores and antique stores for vintage bottles, and check ethnic groceries for modern, foreign bottles. Choose a few, in case one accidentally breaks when drilling.

2. Drill the hole.

This is the hardest part of the process. A hole near the base of the bottle is needed as an exit for the electrical cord. You'll want to put this hole on the back of the bottle, and fortunately most soda bottles give us a little head start, in the form of a D-shaped notch. Place the tip of the masonry/glass drill bit in this little notch, and carefully start drilling. Sometimes a piece of gaffer's tape or duct tape is useful to prevent the bit from slipping.

Drill with steady pressure, resting the bottle in something that will cushion it (those styrofoam things they ship wine bottles in are ideal). Keep nice, steady pressure on the bit, but be wary of leaning too hard on the bottle. Drill in short bursts, allowing the glass to cool between bursts.

Now, the bottles can crack or break, and probably will, if you do enough of these, but the good news is it almost always happens the same way: the base of the bottle snaps off. I've never had a bottle shatter or splinter — just the base of the bottle pops off. Preventing breakage is a matter of being aware of how much pressure you're applying when drilling, letting the bottle cool after bouts of drilling, and generally just being patient.

It's also a good idea to keep a short length of your electrical cord handy so you can test that the diameter of your hole is enough to accommodate the cord. No reason to drill any more than you have to.

3. Feed the electrical cord through the bottle.

Start from the bottom hole you just drilled. Verify that your hole is big enough, has relatively clean, smooth edges, and won't do anything rude like strip the insulation from your cord. Shove the cord up through the bottle and out the top.

4. Install socket and plug end.

Take your candelabra-sized socket and get ready to void its likely nonexistent warranty. First, remove the cardboard cuff that usually sheathes these sockets. If it has 2 long metal legs, break those off by bending them repeatedly. Next, separate the wires on the electrical cord, and strip about ¼" of insulation off the 2 ends. Now loosen the terminal screws on the socket and, making a hook of the stripped wire

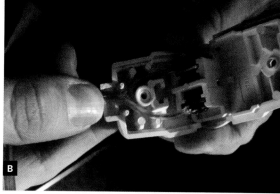

Fig. A: Once the hole is drilled, feed your electrical cord through. Make sure the diameter is big enough not to harm the wire. Fig. B: There are many different designs for plug ends — this type, while bulky, hinges open and makes installation easy. Fig. C: The socket fits surprisingly well in the PVC cuff, and just as well over the tape-covered bottle lip. Fig. D: Once it's all together, make sure the cuff is nice and tight and the lamp sits and balances well.

ends, secure the 2 wires onto the terminals.

Take the other end of the cord, separate the wires, and strip as before. Install the plug end, following the instructions that came with it (different types have different methods).

5. Fit the PVC cuff.

In many ways, this is the crucial part that makes it all possible. Securing the socket in the neck of the bottle was the trickiest issue, and finding just the right way to do it took lots of experimenting. So here's what I figured out: a ¾" slip-fit PVC pipe adapter fits almost perfectly over the mouth of the bottle, and the interior diameter is just about a perfect match for the socket. To ensure that everything fits snugly, wrap the socket and the upper lip of the bottle in a layer of electrical or gaffer's tape. Then, slide the socket into the cuff and fit the cuff over the tape-covered lip of the bottle. It should be a tight fit, so you may need to use a little force.

6. Screw in the bulb, and test. Then wire in your switch.

We'll do a test before we wire up the switch, to make sure all our connections are solid. Screw in the bulb and plug it in. If you have a cheery 40W glow, you've done well and can wire up the switch. If not, check your socket and plug connections, and check your cord for breaks. Once it works, wire your in-cord switch according to the instructions that came with it. Generally, this means separating the wires in a small section of the cord, cutting one of the wires, and fitting the switch over that section with the break. Test the switch.

7. Pick a shade and enjoy!

We like to match the shade to the colors on the bottle's printing, if there is any. You'll want shades designed to clip onto candelabra bulbs, or ones that rest on the PVC cuff.

Once you get your shade, you're done! Stick it on a side table and bask in the glow of trash-born treasure.

Jason Torchinsky is a tinkerer and artist, cofounder of Avacast (avacast.com), a webcasting company, and a member of the Van Gogh-Goghs comedy collective (vgg.com). Sally Myers is a freelance graphic designer, photographer, and is half of Pumpkin Designs, (myspace.com/craftyjewishgirls).

Hand-Carved Crochet Hook

Turn deadwood into a beautiful object you'll have forever. BY JIM PRICE

My dream in life since my dad died in 1953 was to own our old property on Deadman Creek (we say "crick") in Eastern Washington. Happily, in October of 2000 we were able to buy back 30 acres of the place. Now I'm doing what I can to build a cabin to replace our house, which is no longer there. One thing I'm doing to raise funds for the building project is hand-carving wooden crochet hooks out of branch wood I collect from the ranch.

Got a sharp pocketknife? A stick? A little saw and sandpaper? That's about all you need to make a crochet hook with the feel and warmth that you just can't buy at Wally World. So let's make one.

Photograph by Arwen O'Reilly

Fig. A: A good diameter of stick to start with.
Fig. B: This is what a good whittling stick should look like at its core. If it has a soft, pithy core, find a different stick.

Fig. C: Whittle off long, curly shavings, turning the stick as you go. Keep both hands behind the blade.
Fig. D: Sand along the grain of the wood while turning it.

Materials

» **Straight deadwood stick**
» **Pocketknife**
» **100–400 grit sandpaper**
» **Pull saw**
» **Polymerized oil** (optional)

1. Find a good stick.

First thing: go on a hook stick hunt. Saw a straight length 6"–8" from a dead, uncracked hardwood branch that's about twice the diameter of the hook you'd like, something like Figure A.

Heft it in your hand. Picture it as a hook. Look at the stick end. See a soft, pithy core? If so, convince that stick to become a drinking straw and start over.

This time, find a stick that looks more like Figure B, with a tiny, hard center and closely spaced growth rings. The sample chunk in the photos is briar. Fruitwood works well too, as do most hardwoods. Avoid softwoods unless you're planning a really large hook where strength can be in the mass.

2. Get started whittling.

It shouldn't be hands flailing and blade flashing like Cap'n Jack's sword. Carve nice 1"–2" strokes, with your hands arranged as in Figure C.

This is important; you can remove wood quickly, safely, and accurately this way. Also, you're far less likely to cut yourself when both hands are behind the blade. Hold the stick in one hand, and with the thumb of that hand, push against the thumb of the knife-holding hand.

Start whittling back a couple of inches from the future hook tip, and whittle off long, curly shavings, turning the stick as you go. Keep at it until you have a fairly straight 2" shank that's roughly the diameter you want. Go ahead and be enthralled with the beauty of the wood you're uncovering.

3. Smooth the wood.

Now comes the sandpaper. Sand along the grain while turning the blank, to make the hook shank cylindrical (Figure D).

Use progressively smaller grit sizes (starting with 100 and graduating to 400). Sand the hook shank smooth, then whittle and sand a rounded tip to your liking.

Photography by Jim Price

E   F

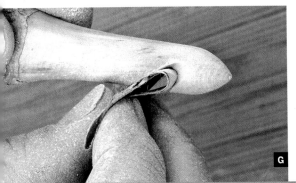

G   H

Fig. E: Make an angled cut set back from the tip. Make sure not to cut too deep. Fig. F: With controlled, shallow cuts, gradually deepen the notch.

Fig. G: Once the notch has been shaped, enlarge it with sandpaper. Fig. H: You're done! You now have a hook that's as beautiful as the things you'll make with it.

If you want a specific, accurate size, use a hook-sizing gauge and keep sanding till the shank fits the gauge hole that matches your desired hook size.

4. Create the hook tip.

Now take your little saw (I like a thin-kerf pull saw for this). Start the cut back from the hook tip, a distance about twice the diameter of the shank (Figure E). Make it an angled cut (45°–60°). Don't cut too deep or you'll be scouting another stick. Cut through no more than half the diameter.

5. Fine-tune the notch.

Gradually carve a bevel down to the bottom of the saw cut (Figure F). Make very short, controlled, shallow cuts, gradually deepening the notch.

Don't try to hack the notch out ninja-style or you'll be out stick hunting again. You should be forming a sharp, angular notch.

6. Finish it up.

Here's the trick: Enlarge and smooth the notch (I call it a gullet) with folded or rolled sandpaper in a seesaw motion (Figure G). Use smaller and smaller grits until the gullet is smooth. You're just about there.

Hold the hook as you would when crocheting, taking note of where your thumb and forefinger rest in relation to that beautifully shaped hook. Now whittle the hook handle, with a thumb flat formed where you noted.

Sand the handle smooth and voilà, you have a crochet hook. Leave it au naturale, or apply a finish. I prefer a polymerized oil, rubbed until it's almost too hot to hold. Then it's done (Figure H).

Crochet!

Jim Price has been making and selling hand-carved and turned crochet hooks to fund construction of the "front porch" on his family ranch in Eastern Washington. See his hook auction and read his story on his blog at jimbosfrontporch.blogspot.com.

Wood Sun Carving

Practice the folk art of woodcarving by making a simple sun. BY KYLE THOMPSON

If the sight of your own blood makes you nauseous, your friends and family fear for their lives when you pick up a sharp object, or you're a hand model for soap ads, this project may not be the right craft for you. On the other hand, if you enjoy a challenge, want to try something new, and are good with Band-Aids, this might be the answer to your next obsession.

I became hooked on woodcarving when I was just a kid. I loved watching my Dad carve faces out of wood from the camphor tree in my Grandma's backyard, and longed to have his skills. At the end of his life, woodcarving was his meditation and his hope for a future during his bout with a terminal disease. Any talent I may have as a woodcarver, I owe to him. This project is dedicated to his memory.

Photography by Susan Thompson

GENERAL SAFETY GUIDELINES

Make sure you have plenty of room. You are using a sharp object to make cuts in wood and are using great pressure to make those cuts. If you're a beginning woodcarver, you *will* slip. You want to make sure you have plenty of room to make a mistake when it happens, and it's best if no one else is around to be in the way. *Make cuts away from your body.*

The sharper the knife, the better. A sharper knife means less pressure is needed to make cuts in the wood. Less pressure means more control over the knife and thus *less* possibility of cutting yourself. A sharp knife also gives the wood a more finished look. There are many books available for learning how to sharpen a knife. Naturally, the more cuts you make, the duller your knife will get, but that's a topic for another article.

Wear protection. One of the best ways to protect against hand and finger injuries resulting from accidental knife slips is by wearing safety gloves made for wood-carvers. Some are made of Kevlar, Spectra, and/or stainless steel and are excellent for cut resistance, durability, softness, and wearability. Although some woodcarvers only use one glove (usually the hand that holds thecarving), it may be wise to wear gloves on both hands when you're making your first attempts at woodcarving.

Be patient. Don't rush. If this is your first time learn-ing to carve, take your time. You are working with sharp objects. Really sharp! And your skin is hardly as tough as the wood you'll be working with.

Materials

- » **Piece of basswood or pine**
  1"×8"×12"
- » **Hand tools for carving,** including palm tools and chisels
- » **Mallet** for hitting chisels
- » **Pencil and paper**
- » **Band saw** (if available)
- » **C-clamp or bench clamp** to hold carving
- » **Wood finish** (optional)
- » **Apron** (optional)
- » **Band-Aids** just in case
- » **Pattern** available online at craftzine.com/04/diywhittleit_sun

BASIC CUTTING TECHNIQUES

These are just a few of the standard cuts you'll be making with your sun carving. There are carving books with many pictures that can help you make the most of your cuts, but I've found the best way to learn how to shape wood is simply by doing it. New woodcarvers should make many practice cuts on a practice piece of wood before beginning this project.

Stop cut: Using a chisel or knife, make a perpendicular cut in the wood that will act as a guide for where you want your knife blade to stop when you're carving. Stop cuts should not go much deeper than ¼" at a time, so you may need to repeat stop cuts until you reach your desired depth. This is the most appropriate time to use a mallet to make your cuts, giving you enough strength to cut against the grain.

Gouging cut: Cutting the wood with a chisel at an angle. Take care that the angle is not too steep, or you may gouge out too much wood at one time. You can use a mallet here, but I would suggest using your body weight instead — it will give you more control.

Beveling/rounding cut: Rounding the wood to give it a curved shape. This is usually done making several small cuts.

✱ **TIP:** Cutting parallel with the grain or perpendicular against the grain are usually the most difficult situa-tions. Cutting with the grain, the tool moves easily, but the grain itself can take you off course due to the curving nature of wood. Cutting against the grain is difficult because of the compact nature of the wood fiber working in direct opposition to your blade. As much as possible, try to cut diagonally across the grain, and you'll have the smoothest results.

✂ RECOMMENDED TOOLS AND MATERIALS

Carving Tools I recommend palm tools and a couple of chisels for this carving. These are good beginner tools for a couple of reasons. They offer more control over the cuts they are making and are also, therefore, safer. One thing to always keep in mind when making cuts in wood: *always make cuts away from your body.*

Wood Basswood and pine are probably the most widely used by woodcarvers who do folk woodcarvings. Basswood is known for its smooth face and small grain, but may be difficult for the beginning woodcarver, because it's a harder wood. Pine is softer, but chips more easily, so the details will be harder to refine. The sun carving in this project is made from basswood.

- -

- 📷 Gallery of carvings: craftzine.com/04/ diywhittleit_sun
- ➕ Kyle Thompson's site: craftzine.com/go/kyle

A

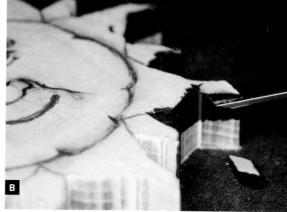

B

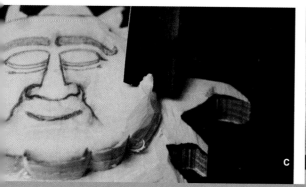

C

D

Fig. A: The pattern transferred to the wood. Notice the pattern changes in the next pictures to make the mouth a little different. Fig. B: Be careful when carving wood from the rays. The less wood you have, the easier it can break or chip off. Fig. C: When rounding, make many small cuts. Smaller cuts equal more control. Fig. D: My left thumb is the pressure behind the blade, while my right hand controls the direction of the knife. Be careful!

Make Your Sun Carving

1. Print and cut out the pattern, then transfer it by firmly tracing the pattern onto the wood. This will leave a light indentation of the pattern on the wood that you can darken in with a pencil if desired. Make sure your pattern goes with the grain of the wood from forehead to chin.

2. Allow room for artistic license when you draw the pattern. Every carving I do turns out a little differently. Allow yourself to make mistakes — it may turn out for the better. Also, feel free to make the pattern as large as your wood allows, which will give you a little more room to deal with potential mistakes.

3. Cut the pattern out of the wood with a band saw. If you don't have a band saw, you may need to simplify the design (e.g., straighter rays, or fewer of them). Alter the design to fit your needs (Figure A).

NOTE: As you carve, work from the perimeter of the drawing to the middle, starting with the sun's rays. Different parts of the sun will lose more layers of wood than others. For example, when finished, the

sun's rays will have the least amount of wood left, while the nose will have the most.

4. Make stop cuts all around the face's perimeter.

5. Using a felt pen, block out the wood you need to cut from the sun rays — a little less than ½" down. Chip the wood away until you've reached the desired depth (Figure B). You need to make several stop cuts to reach this depth. Do not round the sun's rays at this time — you'll need to use the rays to clamp your carving to your workbench. You'll round the rays in the final step in the project.

6. Clamp the wood to your workbench. You may need to change the clamp's placement throughout the project for the best angles of particular cuts.

7. Make bevel cuts all around the circle of the face, leaving the center of the face untouched; leave lots of wood for the chin, nose, and brow (Figure C).

8. You may need to redraw parts of the face as you carve. This helps give you a strong mental image of how you want your final piece to look. Redraw the

E F

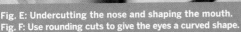

G H

Fig. E: Undercutting the nose and shaping the mouth.
Fig. F: Use rounding cuts to give the eyes a curved shape.

Fig. G: Steep-angled stop cuts hollow out the inside of the mouth. Fig. H: Rounding the sun rays.

eyebrows, then use stop cuts to outline the brows. Make gouge cuts to remove wood around the brows, then shape them with rounding cuts (Figure D).

9. Redraw and carve the nose. Make stop cuts for the nose, the outlines of the top half of the eyes, and the cheek outlines. Using gouge cuts, carve out the area around the nose, the eye sockets, and the area from just above the chin to just below the end of the nose. Shape the nose with rounding cuts (Figure E).

10. Redraw and carve the eyes. Make a stop cut for the outline of the eyes. Cut the wood below the eyes up to the stop cut. Use rounding cuts to give the eyes a curved shape (Figure F). Draw the outline for the eyelid. Make a steeply angled stop cut for the eyelids. Undercut the eyelid stop cut to create the eyelid effect, and carefully chip out the excess wood. Repeat the directions above to create the bags under the eyes.

11. Redraw and carve the cheek outlines. Make stop cuts for the cheeks. Shape the area below the nose. Cut the areas above and below the mouth at an angle, down and away from the lips. Make a stop cut for the mouth. Using steep-angled cuts, cut into the

mouth repeatedly and clean excess wood chips out of the mouth (Figure G). Round out the lips.

12. Redraw and shape the cheeks and chin with rounding cuts.

13. Look at the face of your sun and make any final cuts. Clean up unwanted nicks and cuts, then redraw the lines for the smaller rays. Make stop cuts and carve to the desired depth (Figure H). The small rays are carved away more than the large rays.

14. I prefer not to use a wood finish or stain on my carvings, but they can protect the wood from damage and cracking as it dries out. They can also make your carving more aesthetically pleasing to you — the choice is yours.

A big thanks to my inspirations: My father, Daniel Thompson, as well as Emil Janel, Marv Kaisersatt, and Shawn Cipa.

Kyle Thompson is a high school music director, a father and husband, and a believer in the arts as a means for social, emotional, and spiritual change in the world.

Fistful of Needles

Make a multi-needle felting tool on the cheap.

BY MOXIE

Photography by Moxie

I can't stop needle felting. The addiction metaphor is spookily appropriate when you consider that this craft involves dangerous needles. It's amazing what you can do with the tiniest amount of wool fiber: using a bit of fluff the size of something a friend might pick off your sweater, you can make art. It's all in the relationship between the needle and the fiber.

But creating a large piece of fabric with a single needle can take a long time, delaying the fun, decorative details. It's like being on your way to a big party, but having to stop to have your teeth cleaned on the way. If you use multiple needles, it's easier to satisfy the immediate-gratification baby that lives within us all. The necessary tools can be pricey to buy, but they're really simple to make.

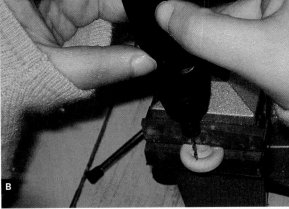

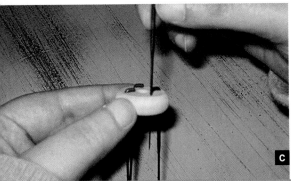
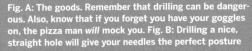

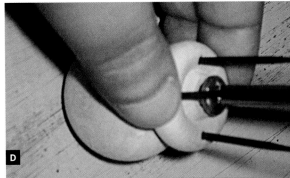

Fig. A: The goods. Remember that drilling can be danger-ous. Also, know that if you forget you have your goggles on, the pizza man *will* mock you. Fig. B: Drilling a nice, straight hole will give your needles the perfect posture for poking. Fig. C: Loading needles into the flat side of the wheel. Fig. D: Get a grip. Make sure you have a good hold on the knob as you screw the pieces together. A slip here could make "fistful of needles" a painful reality.

Materials

» **Drawer pull and wooden wheels**
» **Drill and drill bit** or Dremel tool
» **Screwdriver**
» **Safety glasses**
» **Clamp**
» **Screws** (the drawer pull often comes with screws)
» **Your favorite felting needles**

NOTE: The number of needles you decide to use in your tool is entirely up to you and largely dependent on the types of projects you want to tackle.

1. Drill holes in the wheel.

Secure the wooden wheel in the clamp. Felting needles come in different tip shapes and different gauges. The gauge refers to the length and size of the pokey section of the needle. The radius of the upper portion of the needle will most likely be standard. You may want to drill a test hole to be sure, but most needles will fit well if you use a 5⁄64" drill bit.

A 4-needle tool should provide nice coverage. Determine where to drill your holes. If you want to be picky, you can measure equal distances between the holes you wish to drill. I'm not picky as much as I am lazy, so I went straight to drilling. Don't drill too close to the center hole because it makes it harder to get the screw in later.

2. Assemble!

Insert the needles in the holes in the wheel, with the flat side of the wheel facing the knob. Screw the wheel onto the knob, tightening until the needles stop wiggling.

I've made several tools, each for different tasks. My biggest is a monster with 18 needles. Another has 8 needles tightly packed for detailing. You can even make your own handles using Fimo or Sculpey clay for a fun, personal touch. Happy stabbing!

Moxie believes in the power of the high-five. She lives in Seattle with her husband and 2 bunnies. She will teach anyone to needle felt in exchange for coffee beverages. madebymoxie.com

Embossed Greetings

Add shimmering designs to handmade cards with aluminum foil and some imagination.

BY DIANE GILLELAND

Photography by Diane Gilleland

T hese cards may look expensive, but they're actually made with ordinary aluminum foil — the kind at your grocery store. Just a few dollars buys you enough foil to make dozens of cards, and the process of embossing is quite addictive and fun.

Your junk drawer is probably loaded with embossing tools — ballpoint pens with no ink left, chopsticks, dull pencils. You can even make imprints with your smaller, plastic crochet hooks and knitting needles. And when you're done embossing, you can add some color to your work with permanent markers or alcohol inks.

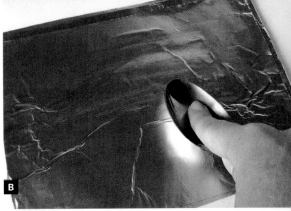

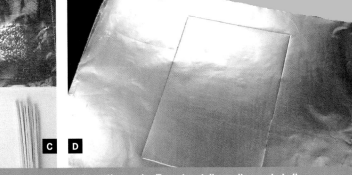

Fig. A: Spread the glue stick evenly over the foil. Fig. B: If your foil gets crinkled while gluing, smooth it out again with the back of a spoon. Fig. C: Test your embossing tools, and see what kinds of lines and textures they make. Try using dull pencils, empty ballpoint pens, wooden chopsticks, toothpicks, and the like. Fig. D: Mark out the area of your finished embossing on your foil using a Sharpie or an embossing tool.

Materials

» **Heavy-duty aluminum foil**
» **Scissors**
» **Glue stick or spray adhesive**
» **Spoon** for smoothing your foil
» **Embossing tools**
» **Padding for your work surface**
  such as an old magazine or sheet of
  craft foam

For transferring a design (optional):
» **Tracing paper**
» **Masking tape**
» **Sharp pencil for tracing**

For adding color to your foil embossing:
» **Sharpie markers in assorted colors
  or alcohol-based inks**
» **Rubbing alcohol**
» **Cotton swabs**
» **Paper towels**

1. Gauge your foil.

You'll need to glue 2–4 layers of foil together, so you end up with a proper thickness for embossing. The number depends entirely on the thickness of your foil (not all brands of heavy-duty foil are created equal!). So start by making a few small swatches: one with 2 layers, one with 3, and one with 4. These only need to be a few inches square. Glue the foil layers together with a glue stick or spray adhesive, and then do a little embossing on each swatch.

Does your embossing tool poke through the foil? Then you need more layers. Does your embossing look soft, with no definition? Then you need fewer layers. Find the number of layers that looks best to you.

2. Test your tools.

Use the swatches you just made to see what kind of embossing you can get out of your various tools. A fine-point pen, for example, incises a very thin line. A blunt pencil makes a thicker line. The blunt end of a chopstick can emboss larger areas. A bundle of toothpicks makes a tiny, stippled texture. Raid your house and see what other embossing tools you can find.

Fig. E: Trace a design onto tracing paper, and then re-trace it onto the foil. Fig. F: The tracing will leave a lightly-embossed guideline on your foil. Fig. G: Press firmly as you emboss, but not so firmly that you tear the foil. Fig. H: Look how much sharper the details of this design become after a little re-embossing on the back of the foil.

3. Prepare your foil.

Now that you know how many layers you'd like, prepare a piece of layered foil that's a bit larger than you want your finished embossing to be. Glue the layers securely together, making sure they're glued at the edges and corners, too. (As you apply the glue stick, be careful that no little blobs get trapped between the layers of your foil. These will show up on your embossing surface.)

If you end up with some wrinkles on the foil after gluing, you can rub the surface with the back of a spoon to smooth it.

NOTE: You can emboss on either the shiny side or the satiny side of your foil.

4. Pad and define your work surface.

Put a little padding down on your work surface, and tape it in place if you wish. With a padded surface, you'll get a much deeper, more defined imprint.

Place your foil sheet on top of the padding. Define the area in which you'd like your finished embossing to be, by drawing a boundary with a Sharpie or with your embossing tool.

5. Transfer your design.

Or not. You may just want to start embossing on your foil in a free-form way. But you can also adapt designs from books, fabrics, wallpaper — anything.

Use a pencil to trace the forms you like onto some tracing paper. Then lay the tracing paper over your foil, and trace over the lines again with the pencil. This will leave a lightly embossed guideline in your foil.

6. Emboss.

Embossing is nothing more than drawing on the foil with your various tools. Press firmly with your tools as you draw on the foil, but not so firmly that you tear it.

As you emboss, flip your work over from time to time. You can do a little fine-tuning on the back. For example, see how the center of this design looks a little nondescript (Figure F)? Just re-emboss it on the back, and voilà! A nice, defined circle (Figure H).

In fact, you might find that you like the look of your work better on the back. And as you practice foil embossing, you might even begin to plan designs that involve embossing parts on the front and parts on the back.

Fig. I: Color with the side of the marker nib and use a light touch to get smooth color coverage. Fig. J: You can also use alcohol inks instead of markers to add color.

Fig. K: Rub the dried ink with an alcohol-soaked paper towel to create an aged look. Fig. L: Mount your finished embossing on a blank card.

7. Add color.

Because foil is nonporous, you'll need to use permanent, alcohol-based markers and inks to add color. Water-based color will just bead up on the surface.

After testing a number of (more expensive) permanent markers, I found that the good old Sharpie performs best. You can color right on your foil, but use a very light touch — if you press too firmly with your marker, it could leave embossed marks on the foil. If you're coloring a large area, you might want to use the side of the marker nib, so you can get smoother color. If you make any stray marks, you can clean them up with a cotton swab dipped in rubbing alcohol.

You can also buy colorful alcohol inks at many art supply stores, and paint them onto your foil. In fact, you can create an aged look by covering your imprint liberally with ink, and letting it dry for 10 minutes. Then wipe the surface lightly with a paper towel moistened with rubbing alcohol. The ink will remain in the recessed parts of the embossing, but will wipe off the raised parts.

Let your color-work dry thoroughly before proceeding to the next step.

8. Mount on cards.

Using scissors, carefully cut out your finished embossing. Spread glue stick over the back, using light pressure so you don't mar your work. The glue stick will tend to collect in the sunken parts of your work, which is exactly what you want — it helps support the embossing. Make sure you get glue on all the edges and corners of your foil.

Mount your foil onto a blank greeting card. Or you can mount it onto a piece of contrasting paper as matting, and then mount that on a card. Or you can cut a window in your card and mount the foil behind it. The possibilities are endless.

Place your card under something heavy, like a big book, for an hour or so while the glue dries. You're done!

Now try using embossed foil to dress up things like gift boxes, book covers, refrigerator magnets, and shrines.

Diane Gilleland produces CraftyPod (craftypod.com), a blog and podcast about making stuff. She also runs DIY Alert (diyalert.com), a web calendar for all the crafty events in her hometown of Portland, Ore.

Snappy Hankies

It's sew easy to turn button-down shirts into crafty hankies that won't blow your budget. Old clothes often hold fond memories long after their styles have come and gone. This project was inspired by a good friend who refused to get rid of his flannel shirts. Rather than sending them to the thrift store, we recycled them into these quick, easy handkerchiefs. This way we can hang on to our past a little longer and look stylish while we're at it.

You will need: Old button-down shirts; serger, sewing machine, or needle and thread; iron (optional); fabric scissors; ruler

1. Cut out a square.

Choose your shirt and cut squares from the flat areas. Flannel and cotton shirts work well. We cut ours to about 12"×12".

2. Reinforce the edges.

If you're using a serger, use your scissors to round the edges of your square. Then, serge around the perimeter. To use a sewing machine or needle and thread, fold in each edge of the square ¼". Then fold in again another ¼". Iron around the edges. Use a straight stitch to sew in place. That's it!

Handkerchiefs are making a comeback. They're Earth-friendly and very fashionable. By making them yourself, you create your very own personalized tissues that can be washed and used again and again.

Trash Fact: The global tissue business is worth more than $30 billion annually. Reusing handkerchiefs reduces the amount of landfilled tissues, which should help wipe your conscience clean.

Illustration by Tim Lillis

Tiffany Threadgould is a design junkie and the author of the *This into That* books. Her business, RePlayGround (replayground.com), sells recycled goods, features DIY projects, and accepts donations of your unwanted items.

BONUS FEATURE!

Maker Faire
IS FOR CRAFTERS

From kids making their own Yoda dolls to the hyperbolic crochet sea creatures that graced the Lion Brand Yarn booth, the crafty side of Bay Area Maker Faire 2007 was bustling in the main Expo Hall. The mood was excitement, whether crafters were participating in the many demos and workshops, or shopping for handmade goods at Bazaar Bizarre.

The CRAFT booth, with its stunning backdrop of Wende Stitt's three-panel Día de los Muertos quilt, was Grand Central for the crafty demos that covered such topics as silk-screening, Gocco printing, crochet, jewelry making, yarn spinning, and sewing. Recycling and green themes ran strong with sustainable fabrics from Ambatalia and popular demos on how to knit T-shirt rugs and refashion thrift-store knits.

The Needle Felting Playground in the CRAFT Corner was the ultimate lounge area, with a constant swarm of people young and old, poking away at their roving while creating such delights as bunnies, fruit, and flowers. All in all, crafters were zooming around trying to soak in all they could before the doors finally closed and Maker Faire became just a warm, fuzzy, and crafty memory.

—*Natalie Zee Drieu*

➕ Captions and slide show at craftzine.com/04/ makerfaire. Don't miss the Southwest Maker Faire in Austin, Texas, Oct. 20–21, 2007. makerfaire.com

Photography by Sam Murphy

Photography by: Sam Murphy (top left), Margot Duane (top right), Jason Forman (center right), and Scott Beale (bottom)

Photography by: Scott Beale (top and bottom left) and Jason Forman (bottom right)

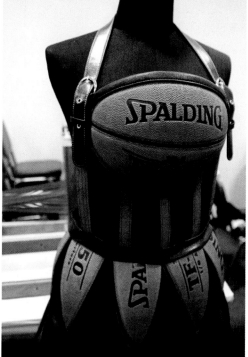

Photography by: Jason Forman (top), Scott Beale (center right), and Margot Duane (center left and bottom)

» *Judith Lange in the studio with natural dye samples.*
The stripes indicate different mordants used.

101:
NATURAL DYEING

By Judith Lange

Everyday plants offer big color.

Photography by Sam Murphy

Imagine a world with no colored fabric. Look in your closet, at your furniture, at your towels and your curtains. Imagine everyone dressed only in white. Such a drab existence does not suit human beings. Long before Rit came in packets, color was everywhere. Beautiful colors were produced from plants, wood scraps, mud, shellfish, even bugs.

My friends and I once spent an entire summer experimenting with natural dyes. It was a fun way to bring more color into our lives; it's sure to be the same for you. Many natural sources of dye are still available today and are simple to use. In this tutorial, I'll show you how to dye wool using the ubiquitous onionskin. This is a grand project for adults and children, singly or in groups (supervise children!).

»

BASICS »

Mordants: Pump Up the Color

Besides natural dyes, *mordants* were used from very early times. Mordants help the dye molecules bond to the fiber and offer a richer color. In other words, mordants help your material to hold the dye and intensify the color. Common examples (and suggested amounts) include:

» **Alum** (2oz/lb of fiber) — Available as a mineral powder, or use an aluminum pot.
» **Iron** (½oz/lb of fiber) — Available as iron sulfate or rust, or use an iron pot, such as a cast iron Dutch oven.
» **Tin** (⅔oz/lb of fiber) — Available as tin chloride.
» **Copper** (⅔oz/lb of fiber) — Use as copper sulfate, or use a copper pot.
» **Chrome** (½oz/lb of fiber) — Use as potassium chromate. When using chrome, please note: ⚠ WARNING! TOXIC – Handle with care.

You can get many good colors using only alum, which is safe to work with and readily available in the spice section of grocery stores.

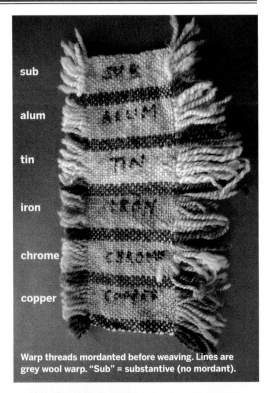

sub
alum
tin
iron
chrome
copper

Warp threads mordanted before weaving. Lines are grey wool warp. "Sub" = substantive (no mordant).

Use a Mordant Before, During, or After the Dyeing Process

Pre-mordant — Dissolve the mordant in 4gal of water (for 1lb. of fiber), add the fiber you'll be dyeing, and simmer for ½–1 hour. You can then put your fiber directly in the dye pot or you can dry it and do your dyeing later.

Mordant during dyeing — Add the mordant to the dye pot along with the dye. Heat to dissolve, add your fiber, and continue heating (at a simmer) for ½–1 hour. This is considered to be less effective than pre-mordanting.

Post-mordant — Simmer water, dye the fiber for ½–1 hour, then add the mordant and simmer for another ½ hour.

NOTE: Unless you are deliberately using an aluminum or iron pot to mordant, use enamel or stainless steel so as not to contaminate the dye.

Some of the author's angora goats (mother and daughter) with sheep in the background.

Some results of our dye experiment and a lot of white wool and mohair.

1. LEARN THE BASIC DYE RECIPE

For a dye bath for ½lb of plant or animal fiber:

• Use about 4gal of water. (If your water has a high mineral content, it may alter the color of the dye. If you care about this, use bottled or distilled water.)

• Add dye matter. Formulas are available online and in many excellent books on natural dyeing (see Resources on page 154). If experimenting, start with equal weights of dye and fiber.

⚠ WARNING! Once you use a pan for dyeing, don't use it for cooking. You can't be sure all plants and minerals are safe.

• Simmer the pot for ½ hour or so to release the color from the plant material, then remove the plant matter. If you leave the plant material in the pot with your fiber, the color may be uneven. If you like variegated color, leave the plant material in!

MATERIALS

» ALUM, 1–2OZ, AVAILABLE AS A MINERAL POWDER, OR USE AN ALUMINUM POT
» WATER, UP TO 4GAL; DISTILLED OR PURIFIED WATER IS PREFERABLE.
» NATURAL FIBER, ½LB, SUCH AS WOOL, OR SOMETHING LIKE A PAIR OF WOOL SOCKS
» ONIONSKINS, ½LB, YELLOW AND/OR RED. ASK YOUR FRIENDLY GROCER IF YOU CAN SCAVENGE THROUGH THE BOTTOMS OF THE ONION BINS.

• Add pre-mordanted fiber and simmer ½–1 hour. Let stand overnight, or remove the fiber at this point.

NOTE: It's impossible to color-match plant dyes. The plants you're using may grow in different soil, weather, and water conditions, and there may be a number of varieties within the species. Fibers also take dyes differently.

2. DYE YOUR YARN WITH ONIONSKINS

So much for the generalities. Now let's dye wool yarn with onionskins (yellow and red mixed).

2a. Mordant the wool in an enamel pot containing 1–2oz of alum dissolved in 2gal of water. Our actual weight of fiber is ½lb. Simmer for ½ hour. Let cool in the liquid, then proceed to dyeing, or let the fiber dry and dye at a later time. You can reuse this water for mordanting more fiber (but not for dyeing).

2b. To prepare the dye pot, place ½lb onionskins in 2gal of simmering water for ½–1 hour. Remove the onionskins, if desired, and then add the mordanted wool (wet or dry) and simmer another ½–1 hour.

2c. Alternatively, place the onionskins and the mordanted wool in 2gal of simmering water, and simmer ½–1 hour. (Skins can be placed in a net bag if desired.)

NOTE: This same procedure can be used for many protein fibers, including wool, mohair, alpaca, llama, rabbit, and dog, and also for most dyes on cotton and linen.

2d. Try other dyes to achieve different colors, such as madder for red and eucalyptus leaves for brown. Yellows, browns, and reds are easy to get, but blues from indigo and woad are more complicated. Many books will suggest different plants to dye with. We did experiments with 50 plants in a summer; Ida Grae's book *Nature's Colors* lists 250. See the next page for more natural dyeing materials.

TIP: The fibers don't need to be white; interesting colors come from naturally colored fibers and from overdyeing previously dyed things.

NOTE: If you are a more casual type of "cook," play my favorite "what if" game, and just throw a bunch of fiber, a bunch of onionskins, and a tablespoon or so of alum together and go with it! Play and see what happens.

3. RINSE AND DRY

3a. Lift your fiber out of the pot, or drain the liquid off.

3b. Rinse the newly dyed fiber with water that's about the same temperature as the liquid you took it out of. Rinse off the excess dye until the water runs clear. Do not agitate the wool.

3c. Air dry (don't use a hot dryer!). Now you're done. Enjoy!

Variations

Mordant some yarn with alum, and some with iron. Then dye them both with onionskins. You will now have 2 colors to work with. If you put more than one color or type of fiber through the same process together, you will have several colors to use together. A vast array of colors can be achieved by overdyeing one color over another, and by using different mordants. Your options are endless. Have fun!

Dyes to Try

» **Rich browns** — walnut hulls, eucalyptus leaves
» **Reds** — madder, cochineal bugs
» **Brilliant yellows** — lichens, safflowers
» **Good yellows** — onionskins with alum
» **Oranges** — coreopsis and onionskins, dahlias with tin and iron
» **Greens** — somewhat difficult to get without overdyeing. Overdye a yellow with indigo. Try using copper or iron as a mordant, which produce an olive green with some natural dyes.

The 2 skeins on the left were dyed using well water that contained iron, along with onionskins and an alum mordant. The roving on the right was dyed using the same process, but with distilled water.

FINISH ☒

⊞ See History and Resources on next page. Go to craftzine.com/04/101 for a list of materials sources.

Judy Lange has been an artist and teacher for most of her adult life. She says her science-and-art background is a lovely mix. Currently, she raises angora goats and sheep for their quality of fiber; teaches spinning, felting, and dyeing; and sells yarn, fiber, and animals. Her favorite question is "What happens if …?"

HISTORY »

Dyeing Throughout History

Natural dyeing was a common profession through much of history, and in Europe, the dyers of red cloth were literally in a class by themselves. Some other interesting facts:

» **Woad** was used by Celtic warriors to paint their bodies blue to scare their enemies. In wool and weaving industries, woad was used as a dye fiber. It became a major crop in medieval Europe, and later in colonial America.

» **Indigo**, grown in India for 4,000 years, gave a more intense dye but was much more expensive. It was banned from Europe to protect woad farmers.

» Red, the color of royalty, was not available to ordinary folks because of its rarity and cost. **Madder** roots, which give a strong red, became a main source of wealth in Europe during the Middle Ages. At its peak in the 1800s, world production was 70,000 tons, with Britain spending £1,000,000 a year to import a third of the total. Redcoats, anyone?

» **Cochineal**, from a Mexican insect used by the Aztecs, was a major source of income for the Spanish after they conquered Mexico. They exported the bugs to Europe for brilliant reds. ✄

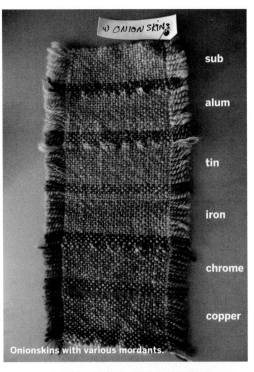
Onionskins with various mordants.

sub
alum
tin
iron
chrome
copper

RESOURCES

My county library has 24 books on natural dyes, with some useful information in all of them. These are a few favorites:

Nature's Colors: Dyes from Plants by Ida Grae, Macmillan Publishing 1974, Collier Books 1979, Robin & Russ Handweavers 1991, out of print. A very good book.

A Dyers Garden: From Plant to Pot, Growing Dyes for Natural Fibers by Rita Buchanan

Dye Plants and Dyeing: A Handbook by the Brooklyn Botanic Garden, a special printing of *Brooklyn Botanic Garden Record: Plants and Gardens* Vol. 2, 1969. I have the 9th printing, 1973.

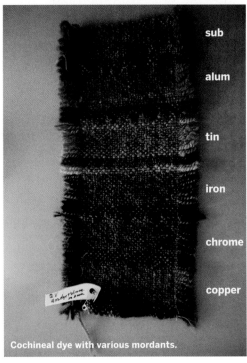
Cochineal dye with various mordants.

sub
alum
tin
iron
chrome
copper

Susie Bright
Susie's Home Ec

» Susie Bright is an amateur dressmaker and a professional writer. She blogs at susiebright.com.

Life's Too Short for Pants

The modern woman endures a lifetime love affair with pants. The tears will come, as well as the joys.

It started off in that golden period, between John Lennon announcing the Beatles were more popular than Christ, and the first copy of *Ms. Magazine* appearing on our doorsteps. Across the fruited plain, in every school, grade, and class, a voice announced on the public address system: "Next Monday, girls will be allowed to wear pants." Often, there was a postscript: "Dungarees will not be tolerated."

The next school day, every female appeared on campus in trousers, leggings, and yes, dungarees (that is to say, *jeans*). There was only one hitch: it's difficult to look great in pants. Trouser-liberators like Kate Hepburn were a rail-like exception to the rule.

Jeans were made originally for men to work in, at manual labor. There wasn't a lot of call for making one's derrière look fabulous. Most men would just as soon live with plumber's butt and jackets that cover it all up. Early tailors never thought about making jean designs that held you in the right places and let you out in the others.

Of course that's all changed now. You walk into a typical jeans store, and they have walls of folded denim and khaki, with signs directing you to styles like "curvy," "low rise," "classic," "relaxed," "boy cut," and the enigmatic "long and lean" — is that an aspiration or a current appraisal?

Whatever their euphemisms, after a frantic couple of hours in the dressing room, you're sweating like a mule and anything but "relaxed." Every pair looks dreadful. You've either got camel toe, or you're swimming — a sad stick figure, or the broad side of a sagging barn. Perhaps a 10-year-old child *would* look good in their "boy cut."

But you — you are crafty. You slam the door behind those stupid gauchos and give the rebel yell: "I'm making my own pants, you sons of bitches!"

And this is where the lycra-denim meets the road, ladies. You're going to find out that the reason ready-to-wear jean sizing is a bottomless pit of frustration is because: a) pants must be individually tailored to fit properly, with a first draft and then a final cut, because your bottom is as tricky as a thumbprint; and b) the female form — in which your hips or breasts are wider than your dead center — *looks* better in a skirt.

Oh, please don't tell Gloria Steinem I told you this. You'll still play kickball, hoe a field, and mine for gold far more effectively in dungarees. But your personal appearance will be *flattered* by a skirt or dress that flows over your hips, rather than cradles them.

If you are a beginning sewer, the first thing you must do when you vow to make your own pair of jeans is to purchase a simple pattern for a *straight-grain, A-line skirt*. Long, short, slit, seamed — try them all. Kwik Sew has a wrap-around skirt, #2954, that virgins could sew on their first thread-and-needle outing.

The secret is this: you cut the size that closely matches your fullest hip-area measurement. That might be your belly, your pube line, or your thighs, but whatever the wide point is, *that's* your magic number. *Ignore* the listings of waist sizes; it all gets adjusted from the hip. That one hip measure, in a skirt, is your guide, as opposed to a pair of jeans, where you'll need a ledger to track all your tailoring notes.

Once you've made your first, second, and third A-line skirts, your ego-to-ass ratio will soar to undreamed-of heights. You'll feel mighty liberated. You'll laugh as you walk past The Gap, "Don't cry for me, Levi Strauss!" You'll also have the sewing experience that will lend you the serious patience and grand perspective it takes to make your first pair of beautifully fitted, great-feeling dungarees. ✂

■ Go to craftzine.com/04/bright for the full article.

In my next column: How to make your first pair of perfect jeans in under two weeks.

BAZAAR

CRAFTY GOODS WE ADORE. *Compiled by Natalie Zee Drieu*

Susan Todd Designs Recycled Bag Collection

$72–$90

susantodd.com

These roomy recycled-sweater tote bags by Susan Todd Designs are so cute, you'll find yourself using them every day to tote around your latest craft projects and daily essentials. Todd rescues sweaters from the salvage shop and creates fun bags in a variety of sweater colors and patterns. The bags' signature fastener is a vintage button that sits on top of a colorful felted wool flower. Multiple interior pockets circle the inside and keep contents in order. Snatch them up in a variety of sizes and styles!

Russell+Hazel Mini Pattern Binder

$16

russellandhazel.com

I always have more than a few craft projects going on at a time, from knitting to crochet to sewing. These mini pattern binders from Russell+Hazel are the perfect pretty place to hold them all, while still being compact enough to stash in my tote bag. The dry erase board in the interior is a major paper saver, letting you jot down quick notes or do on-the-spot math calculations. Use the colorful tabs to separate projects, add pocket holders for special patterns or inspirational images, and finish it off with cool grid paper to design your next craft project.

The Fabric Organizer ⌃

$1–$1.70

thefabricorganizer.com

I got tired of my fabric stash constantly getting disheveled inside my large plastic bin. I always ended up spending a couple hours refolding everything. With the Fabric Organizer boards, each piece of fabric folds perfectly over the durable corrugated plastic, which can hold from ½ to several yards. You'll find cutting and measuring fabric much easier. I also love being able to get an easy, quick glance at my complete fabric stash without having to dig through my bin. (*TIP: Line them up on a bookcase!*) The boards are sized 10"×14" and, for all you quilters out there, there's a convenient 5"×14", which can hold fat quarters or smaller pieces of fabric. It makes you feel like you have a mini fabric store inside your house!

Sew E-Z Boards

$30 for 18"x24", $50 for 33"x51"

joann.com

One of the top commandments of knitting and crochet, which I never followed for years, is to block your work. In the end, I paid the price of uneven knit pieces that had to be sewn together. Nowadays, I don't know what I'd do without my Sew E-Z board. It's so easy to just pin your knitted pieces on the board and spritz with water until they dry. Hours later, the pieces are magically all even! These boards are fantastic because they also work well as a large measuring board, and as an ironing board. Plus, for you space-conscious crafters, they fold up nicely to fit in a closet or under the bed.

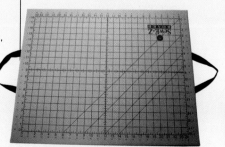

Vickie Howell Yarn Collection: Craft, Rock, and Love

vickiehowell.com/yarn.html

Knit gal extraordinaire Vickie Howell, host of DIY Network's *Knitty Gritty*, has a new yarn collection called Craft, Rock, and Love. The eco-friendly, colorful yarns are made up of a number of different natural fibers. The Craft line is 35% milk fiber and 65% organic cotton, with colors named after beloved crafters. Rock is 40% soysilk, 30% fine wool, and 30% hemp with color names from favorite rock stars. And finally, Love is 70% bamboo and 30% silk, with color names of famous movie couples. A must-have addition to your yarn stash!

Betz White Cup O Joe Pincushion Kit

$18
betzwhite.com

Another cup, please! In fact, make this one a cute, felted-sweater coffee cup. Betz White's Cup O Joe kit lets you make one of her famous pincushions she taught Martha how to make earlier this year. Each kit includes: felted sweater pieces, felted I-cord trim, two heart-shaped pins, six pearly pins, and complete instructions and patterns — all inside a cute white coffee bag. Makes a great gift!

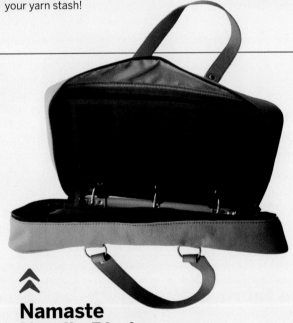

Namaste Needle Binder

$64
namasteneedles.com

Keep all your knitting needles, crochet hooks, and other crafty notions organized in one handy binder that also doubles as a bag. Each needle binder comes with four different "pages": a zippered utility pocket, circular needle pockets, small straight-needle holders, and large straight-needle holders. Extra pages are available at just $7 per. The bags come in chocolate with light blue, avocado with pink, and camel with red, and they zip up for easy storage and portability when you need it on the go.

« Pretty in Punk: 25 Punk, Rock, and Goth Knitting Projects

By Alyce Benevides and Jacqueline Milles $20
chroniclebooks.com

Nothing will be more hip this winter than snowboarding in a mohawk hat or sporting felted camouflage lace-up arm warmers. Whether you're a rebel, rockabilly, goth, or girly girl, stylish knitters can finally rejoice with *Pretty in Punk*'s lineup of designs inspired by punk legends and fashion icons such as John Galliano. —*NZD*

« Bend-the-Rules Sewing: The Essential Guide to a Whole New Way to Sew

By Amy Karol $15
amykarol.com

Amy Karol's craft blog Angry Chicken is one of my daily reads. Karol's new book, *Bend-the-Rules Sewing*, showcases her sewing know-how and veteran tips in the familiar, friendly, conversational style I've come to enjoy. Fabulous vintage fabrics adorn the projects, making it the perfect eye candy that's quite drool-worthy. You learn the basics of sewing while also making up quick gifts, bags, baby clothes, and home décor. —*NZD*

« Just for the Frill of It: 25 Flirty, Fabulous Styles to Make from Clothes You Already Own

By Sonya Nimri $13
watsonguptill.com

The word *frill* had me worried that this book might be too froufrou for my taste, but au contraire — Nimri's style is lacy in a vintage, punk kind of way. Her user-friendly projects show how to chop and sew old tops into fresh and funky new duds. My favorite: a Vivienne Westwood-style cardigan made from an old V-neck sweater and plaid skirt. A must-read before heading for the Goodwill. —*Carla Sinclair*

« Wreck This Journal

By Keri Smith $11
us.penguingroup.com

If you're the type who cringes at the thought of ripping pages, scribbling nonsense, or getting dirty, this book is for you. Dedicated to perfectionists, *Wreck This Journal* is an invitation to break taboos and play on every page. The idea is that once you're done eating colorful candy to make a "tongue painting," or collecting pocket lint with the intent of gluing it in, your eyes will be opened to the boundless joys of creative destruction. —*Goli Mohammadi*

CHECKER BAG

Turn your garbage
into game play.

By Tiffany Threadgould

Photography at left by Sam Murphy; at right by Tiffany Threadgould

MATERIALS

- » **Plastic bottle caps (24)**
  12 each of 2 different colors
- » **T-shirts (2)** in contrasting colors
- » **Fabric scissors**
- » **Ruler**
- » **Shoelaces or cord** for drawstring
- » **Safety pin, straight pins**
- » **Sewing machine**
- » **Iron-on interfacing and iron**
  (optional)
- » **Permanent markers and stickers**
  (optional)

Most items are useful far beyond their first life. It's often just a matter of finding them a new purpose. A pile of garbage can be a crafter's gold mine, and it's easy on the wallet. In this project we'll show you how to transform a pile of plastic caps and 2 T-shirts into a game that will flip your lid!

Lids are hard items to recycle because they're usually of a different grade of plastic than the bottles they cap. It actually helps recyclers to remove bottle lids before recycling. Instead of discarding them, we'll keep them in check and turn them into game pieces. (If you're wondering what your community recycles, visit earth911.org.)

When it comes to T-shirts, most of us have more than we'll ever wear. Just because they're stretched out or stained doesn't mean they're done for. With a few snips and stitches we'll convert them into a brand new game board that doubles as a pouch.

Recycled game play doesn't have to end with this checker bag. For more easy do-it-yourself projects check out *Garbage Games* in the *This into That* books series (replayground.com).

Tiffany Threadgould sells recycled goods, features DIY projects, and accepts donations of your unwanted items.

1. COLLECT YOUR CHECKERS

Collect and clean 12 caps each of 2 different colors. We used caps from orange juice cartons, but you can find them on soda bottles, milk cartons, and other beverages. If you're feeling extra crafty you can decorate the inside of the lids with permanent markers or stickers for when your pieces are "kinged."

✻ IDEA: Use your crafty skills to convert your checkers into chess pieces. Use stickers or markers to decorate the lids into pawns, rooks, knights, bishops, kings, and queens.

2. TAKE MEASUREMENTS

Measure the width of your widest lid, then multiply it by 8. This will be the length and width of your square playing board. Add 2" to the board measurement to determine the pouch width, and add 3" for the pouch length.

Example: Our lids are 1¼" wide
1¼"×8 = 10" square game board
10"+2" = 12" width of pouch
10"+3" = 13" length of pouch

3. CUT THE POUCH

Cut 1 panel from each T-shirt, to the pouch width and length determined in Step 2.

4. CUT THE CHECKERBOARD SQUARES

Take one of the T-shirts and cut 24 squares the same size as the diameter of the lid you measured in Step 2.

5. MAKE THE CHECKERBOARD

Take the panel contrasting in color from the squares you cut, and lay it on a flat surface. Arrange the squares in a checkerboard pattern. Center the pieces on the panel, leaving an extra inch along the length for the drawstring. Either pin the squares in place or iron them on with iron-on interfacing to keep the pieces from shifting.

6. SEW THE BOARD

Using a zigzag stitch on your sewing machine, sew along the edges of the squares.

7. CREATE THE POUCH

Place the 2 fabric panels with the right sides facing in. Sew around 3 sides of the perimeter, leaving the side with the extra inch open.

8. MAKE A DRAWSTRING CASING

Fold the open edge down ¾" and pin in place. Sew a ½" hem along this open edge. Cut 2 small slits in the hem directly across from each other. Be careful not to cut past the hem line.

9. CREATE THE DRAWSTRING

Take one of your cords and attach a safety pin to the end. Thread the cord through a hemmed edge of the pouch, beginning and ending at the same point. Remove the safety pin and tie the ends into a double knot. Repeat this step with a second cord or lace on the opposite side. Once you've secured the second cord with a double knot, pull the drawstrings away from each other, and you've created your game pouch. ✕

GAME PLAY

Object **Capture all of your opponent's pieces or block them so they can't be moved.**

Setup **Take 12 game caps of one color and choose a side of the game board. Place these caps on the first 3 rows on one color of squares. The other player should do the same with his/her caps. All caps should be on the same colored squares.**

Moving **Checkers are moved diagonally forward, one square at a time, toward the other player's side of the board, staying on the same color of square at all times.**

Capturing **You can capture an enemy checker by hopping over it. Capturing, just like moving, is done diagonally. You have to jump from the square directly next to your target, and land on the square just beyond it. Your landing square must be vacant. You can capture more than one piece on a single move as long as the jumping checker has a vacant landing spot available for each capture. When you capture your opponent's piece, remove it from the board.**

Kings **If you can get a checker to the last row on your opponent's side of the board, that checker is flipped over and becomes a king. Now it can move or capture going in either direction — forward or backward.**

Ending the game **The game is won by the first player to capture or block all 12 opposing pieces.**

Brittanie Hoofard
Old School

>> Brittanie Hoofard is a writer and crafter currently living in Korea. In September, she'll get her black belt in taekwondo.

Crocheted Cocktail Rings

I **never met my Great-Grandma Ogilvie. She died** when my mom was young, and the only relics I had of hers were a black-and-white photograph of her in cat-eye glasses, a stack of handmade doilies, and two crocheted cocktail rings.

My mother gave me the rings when I was a teenager, saying, "Grandma Ogilvie used to make these all the time. They became very popular in the 70s." I wore those rings almost every day, tying knots in the elastic, which had years ago lost its give. None of the women in my family knew how to crochet, so when the rings became too fragile to wear, I was unable to find replacements for them.

In the years since, I have scoured thrift stores and antique malls, hoping to find another ring like the ones I wore, or at least a pattern. I eventually taught myself to crochet in hopes of replicating the rings I had as a teen. Recently, I stumbled across a similar pattern on a now-defunct website. The following is my modification of the pattern. ✂

>> **1.** String 25 beads, sized 4mm–6mm, on metallic elastic thread. You can dab clear nail polish on the end of the thread to make it stiff. Keep a little bit of tension on the thread — not completely loose, but not stretched to capacity. There is no gauge for this ring because it's mostly trial and error. My ring was worked with a size 5 hook.

2. Chain 4, and join with slip stitch to form ring.

3. *Slip a bead down, single crochet into ring, repeat from * 4 times, for a total of 5 sc. Make sure the beads are not too loose or tight. They should be flexible, but they also need to stay in place on their own.

4. Make 2 sc, without beads, in each sc of the previous round (10 sc).

5. *Slip bead down, sc in each sc, repeat from * around (10 sc).

6. Sc in each sc (10 times) without beads.

7. Repeat round 5.

8. Repeat round 6.

9. Chain 20 stitches (more or less, depending on the size of your finger) and join with slip stitch to the previous round to form a ring. Turn, slip stitch into each chain stitch, fasten off, leaving a 6" tail.

10. Pull tail through the center of the 5 beads crocheted in round 3. String an extra bead onto tail, pull back through center hole, tie off securely inside bead cluster.

Photograph by Brittanie Hoofard

Betz White
Recycle It

>> Betz White is the author of the upcoming book on recycled felting *Warm Fuzzies: 30 Sweet Felted Projects*. An avid felter, sewer, and green crafter, Betz sells her one-of-a-kind recycled wool items internationally, teaches workshops, and maintains a popular blog at betzwhite.com.

Sweatermorphosis

Refashion your old sweaters into fabulous, no-sweat creations.

Summer's here! Time to take a closer look at the old sweaters accumulating like dust bunnies in the back of your closet. Ask yourself, are you really going to wear that oversized tunic again? Be realistic: if that turtleneck was too itchy to wear last winter, won't it still be too itchy next winter? Try looking at those sweaters as raw materials for some new crafty projects. Use this as an opportunity to challenge your creativity. Make new from old, with the result being one-of-a-kind (not to mention free!).

Start by acknowledging what you still like about your formerly loved sweater. Is it outdated but made with a great yarn? Consider unraveling it and reusing the yarn by knitting or crocheting it into something new.

Is it pilly and misshapen but beautiful in color? Try cutting it into strips to craft with. Did your favorite wool sweater go through the wash and become a Shrinky Dink? Sounds like it's time to cut and sew with sweater felt.

RIP IT GOOD

To recycle yarn, look at the condition and quality of the yarn. If the sweater is heavily worn or partially felted, it won't unravel well and the yarn may have weak spots. Check the seams to see if the sweater is linked together with yarn and not serged seams. (If it was serged together with thread, the pieces were cut and sewn in manufacturing. Avoid this, or you'll end up with short lengths of yarn rather than a continuous strand.)

With the sweater inside out, cut and remove linking yarns. Remove any neck treatment and sleeves. Try to begin unraveling the sweater from the top, as most sweaters are knit from the bottom up. For more tips about unraveling, washing, and winding your recycled yarn, check out this handy link: az.com/~andrade/knit/thrifty.html.

> ### ⟫ *Felting vs. Fulling*
>
> *Felt is an unconstructed fabric (not woven or knit, like a sweater) made of wool fibers bonded together. In the presence of heat, moisture, and friction, wool fibers shrink and bond together resulting in a thick, dense material. When these conditions are applied to a constructed fabric, the process is technically called **fulling**, though in the crafting world (and in this article), most folks still refer to it as **felting**.*

SPIRAL CUT

If you've got a fine-gauge sweater that's too tedious to unravel, try cutting it into "yarn." Starting at the bottom of the sweater, cut off any ribbing or hemming. From the side seam, begin cutting across the sweater, creating a strip about ¼"–½" wide. Make your strips as long as possible by spiral cutting or cutting "in the round" all the way up to the underarms.

Start again at the bottom of each sleeve (remove cuffs first), knotting the ends of the new strips together. Wind your new yarn into balls as you cut. As you might imagine, you can use rather large knitting needles (#19), and projects knit up fast. Any fiber content is suitable, although you might consider the end result before choosing your materials. Soft, absorbent cotton makes a nice bathmat. Silk knits up nicely into a pretty tank top. Count on using several sweaters, depending on the size of your project.

FELT, CUT, AND SEW

Hands down, the most versatile (and my personal favorite) sweater recycling technique is felting. Fiber content first! Start with a sweater that is 100% wool or close to it. Small amounts of other animal fibers, such as angora or mohair, combined with the wool, are acceptable. As a guide, the more stringent the care label (i.e., dry clean only) the better it will felt. Wash the sweater in the washing machine on hot with detergent, and dry on low.

Now that you have your felt, it can be cut without unraveling. It can be sewn with minimal seam allowances. And, the best part is that it can be steamed into submission! Sewing felted wool is very forgiving, even of the wobbliest seams.

A. REFASHIONED SHRUG

This project can be made with almost any sweater of any content, felted or otherwise. (I prefer felted wool as it is less likely to unravel, and a more finished look can be achieved after steaming.) Make sure the shrug's armholes are big enough to accommodate not only your arms, but whatever sleeves you might want to wear under it.

Start by cutting the sweater straight up the center front. Try it on and mark the desired body and sleeve lengths with a pin or two. Keep in mind that you'll be adding back a little length when finishing the raw edges with ribbing. Remove the sweater and cut off the excess body and sleeve lengths where marked.

Cut off the original neckline, smoothing out the curves into the center front cut.

To finish the neckline, I used the ribbing left over from the bottom edge of the original sweater. Pin the ribbing, right sides together, around the new neckline, and stitch. Repeat for sleeve cuffs and the bottom edge of the shrug. Most likely, you won't have enough

A few strategic cuts can transform most any sweater into a cute cover-up. Add decorative buttons for color, and feel free to play around with different trims.

rib from one sweater. This is your chance to mix it up and borrow ribbing from another sweater. Experiment with different color combinations and closures. Finish with a button and buttonhole at the waist, add a tie, or leave it free and easy.

✳ **TIP:** Stretch the ribbing slightly as you pin. This will help ease the body fabric into the rib as you sew.

B. FELTED FAIR ISLE BAG

This next design is inspired by a bag made by Carole Hallman, a participant in one of my felting workshops.

Photography by Betz White

LEFT: Turn this so-so Fair Isle sweater into a surprisingly cute handbag. RIGHT: If you've got it, use it. Start with a hood and you're halfway there!

Begin with a classic, wool, Fair Isle yoked sweater. Throw all care-label caution to the wind and shrink it up in your washer as noted on the previous page. Pin the front to the back along the yoke edge and sew the front and back together. This creates the bottom of the bag. Cut away the sleeves and bottom of the sweater about 2" below the new seam. Make snips perpendicular to the seam to create fringe.

The sweater's neckline becomes the bag opening. Mine had a turtleneck, so I cut it off and hemmed it toward the inside. For a handle, use a long sweater scrap folded lengthwise so the edges meet in the center. Zigzag-stitch down the middle, sewing through all layers. Attach the handle at the sides of the opening. Add a button and cord loop for closure. I also added a removable felted brooch for extra detail. (For my felted brooch tutorial, go to betzwhite.com/blog/2007/01/felted-brooch-tutorial.html.)

C. KIDS' HOODED SCARF
Did your wool hoodie meet an untimely felting fate when it got mixed up with the wrong crowd (that would be the machine-washable laundry)? Revive it with this super-quick project, the Kids' Hooded Scarf! Snip that tiny hood off of the shrunken wool hoodie. Try it on a child to be sure it will fit the recipient. To make the scarf portion, cut a few long rectangles from the sleeves and body, the same width as one side of the hood. Piece together the ends of the rectangles by seaming them with a wide zigzag stitch. Seam each side of the scarf to each side of the hood.

Now that you're armed with tips, techniques, and inspiration, no secondhand sweater is safe! For even more projects and inspiration, check out my upcoming book, *Warm Fuzzies: 30 Sweet Felted Projects*, due out December 2007. ✕

QUICK CRAFT # Candy Box Purses

Some teenage friends of mine were suffering from the purse tyranny of their middle school when we came across these Japanese candy boxes. A glue gun and some fake fur later, we had made these clever recycled purses.

You will need: Japanese candy box, butter knife, clear contact paper or access to a laminating machine, scissors, pencil, hot glue gun, hot glue, Velcro closure, decorative trim, and fake fur (or other material) for lining and strap

1. Deconstruct.

Carefully open the package using the butter knife to keep the flaps from tearing. Lay the package flat and press the design side onto clear contact paper. Trim. *For a more durable purse, have it professionally laminated. Kinko's charges $3 per square foot.*

2. Add lining.

Fold the flaps up and trace the center shape onto the lining. Cut the lining to cover the center, and glue down on the inside of the box.

3. Attach handle.

Glue the handle to the ugly side of the cardboard, folding the flaps over to secure them.

4. Reconstruct.

Reconstruct the box and re-glue on the original seams. Attach Velcro closure and trim. Enjoy!

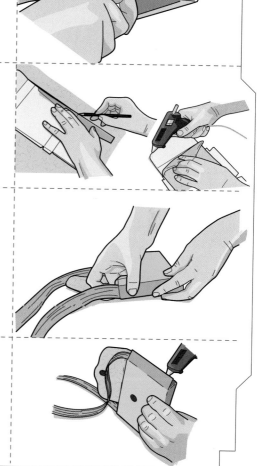

Photograph by Karl Schaefer; illustrations by Tim Lillis

Racelle Rosett is a television writer who has won the Writer's Guild Award and a national cupcake decorating contest, and whose recipe was "February" in last year's Empire Kosher chicken calendar.

Wendy Tremayne
Re: Fitted

» Wendy Tremayne lives in Truth or Consequences, N.M., where she is renovating an RV park into a 100% reuse off-grid B&B called Green Acre. One of her projects, Swap-O-Rama-Rama, is a community clothing swap and series of DIY workshops designed to offer people an alternative to consumerism. Check out gaiatreehouse.com and swaporamarama.org.

Plastik Wev: A Playful Journey in the Web of Public Space

I met artists **Blanka Amezkua and Lina Puerta** as a pair, as friends. First I observed their similarities: courageous use of materials, explosive color, and an unbounded approach to making things. Later I was able to see their distinct artistic voices. But I was particularly drawn to their similarities and wondered what spawned the vibrancy they have in common. First I noticed the obvious: cultural histories, art made for public spaces, and teaching. A deeper look revealed their mutual understanding of reciprocity in which creativity is borrowed, shared, and returned to its source.

Amezkua and Puerta share a migrant experience. At similar stages of life they each moved back and forth between two countries. While they both currently reside in New York, Amezkua has lived in Mexico, and Puerta in Colombia. Their lives outside the United States spawned a particular ease about reusing materials. Amezkua found a desire to create in Mexico, where there was no awareness regarding recycling and the weakening environment. "You did it because you simply had to," she says.

But it's not just that their materials have had a previous life. Through these artists, an object becomes embodied. Puerta refers to her materials as "immortal." Amezkua sees hers as "imbedded with a distinctive power ... It's already been touched, handled, and caressed by many other hands. Perhaps even the environment has manipulated its intention via wind, dirt, or rain." Her role in the object's life is "bestowing it with new interpretation."

By creating art for public spaces, the artists release these newly embodied materials into the community, where objects transform into experiences. Amezkua sees this as the placing of "an idea within a world of ideas." By teaching their discoveries to children, they insure that the life they set in motion will have longevity.

These two artists understand a great deal more than how to make something. What they've discovered is nature's process of creativity. They know that imagination is not the property of an individual or even a generation or culture. It is not bound to a particular time — it is made by the human community, timeless and even immortal if one knows how to give it flight.

Puerta and Amezkua created *Plastik Wev* to demonstrate that transformation could be extended beyond materials that have been reused. They have placed Wevs in their native landscape, adorning stairwells, gates, fences, and tree trunks in New York City. Wevs set in motion a kind of play between maker and public while encouraging consideration of the all-encompassing web — the one that contains all life on Earth — asking us all to reflect on the delicate nature of our interdependence. ✕

A. Cut.
Gather plastic bags, place them on the floor or a table, and cut along their sides, removing the handles. Cut to create long rectangles.

B. Roll.
Make long plastic strands by rolling the rectangular plastic into strips.

C. Shape and Wev.
Create shapes by knotting and folding the strips in any pattern desired. Use pipe cleaners to fasten and make joints.

D. Transform.
Fasten one shape to another with pipe cleaners to form the Plastik Wev. Now, place the Wev within a landscape to transform it.

A

B

C

D

ABOVE: Wevs adorn trees (top) and stairwells (bottom), in New York City, where artists Blanka Amezkua and Lina Puerta currently live.

Photography by: Blanka Amezkua (left column), Lina Puerta (right column)

ハウー
チューンズ

SPRING-LOADED CHOPSTICKS

DŌMO ARIGATŌ, TUCKER-SAN.

USE CHOPSTICKS AND CLOTHESPIN.

REPLACE WOOD OF CLOTHESPIN WITH CHOPSTICKS.

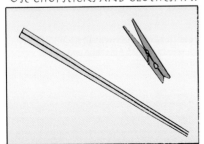

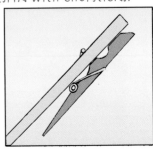

HOWTOONS.COM

BAKA
MO
ICHI-
GEI.

SPRING-LOADED CHOPSTICKS HAVE MANY USES SUCH AS EATING UTENSILS AND TWEEZERS.

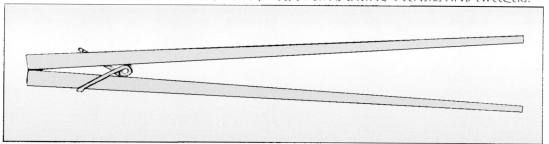

NICK DRAGOTTA · JOOST BONSEN · SAUL GRIFFITH

FREE PATTERNS!
www.OzarkHandspun.com

Ozark Handspun
Artisan-crafted, hand-dyed natural yarns available
in hundreds of locations nationwide.
Ask at your local yarn shop.

POSTAGE
ALPHA STAMPS
CENT
WWW.ALPHASTAMPS.COM

kiku
handmade

www.kiku-co.com

**Submit YOUR freeWILDTHING and you
could win cool prizes or even CA$H !!!!**

[go to freewildthings.com/submit for details]

FREE WILDTHINGS!
freewildthings.com

FREE WILDTHINGS!
freewildthings.com

WILD GINGER
FREE WILDTHINGS!
SOFTWARE, INC
freewildthings.com

" WE think one of the best things in life is still free."

freewildthings.com

namaste glass™
inspirational glasswork

pendants

buckles

wine bottle stoppers & more

www.namasteglass.net

THE CRAFTY SCIENTIST

Fun and funky, recycled and repurposed goods for you and your pets!

Experimental designs just for you!

craftyscientist.com

AMAZING MAGNETS

RARE EARTH MAGNETS

Discs, Rods, Cubes, Plates, Spheres, Rings and Blocks
Great for Crafts & Hobbies
Snaps, Catches, Latches, Name Tags, Modeling, and Science Experiments!

WARNING—Rare earth magnets are very powerful and can easily pinch fingers. Not to be used as a toy.

www.amazingmagnets.com

© 2006 Amazing Magnets, LLC

Fancy Schmancy

custom jewelry & handmade toys

WE LIKE YOU.

www.fancyjewels.com   www.schmancytoys.com

WE GIVE YOU THE TOOLS TO MAKE A DIFFERENCE

firstgiving

www.firstgiving.com

ONLINE FUNDRAISING FOR EVERYBODY

ifm
INTERNATIONAL FASHION MACHINES

design products tech kits

electronic textiles

www.ifmachines.com

© 2007 International Fashion Machines, Inc. All Rights Reserved

Recycled Beer Glasses

Mmmmm, beer!

www.elsewares.com

Marketplace from Etsy.com

wish you were here?
sign up at www.etsy.com

Knitting
fringe $64

Jewelry
jNicDesigns $17

Holiday
moxiephotodesign $3

Ceramics & Pottery
purplepetunia $30

Weddings
heatherjeany $325

Furniture
Paulus $1790

Clothing
liinok $48

Candles
aromaticbodyoils $9

Geekery
GeekGear $24.99

Clothing
ParableInk $48

Bags & Purses
Jmacc $42

Housewares
rubyfaz $4.50

Housewares
UniqueLighting $30

Clothing
xenosdesigns $42

Accessories
therage $120

Supplies
WhiteWillow $16

Etsy seller: stiksel

"I just want to create things that I like and have fun
making them. I think that is my goal right now; I enjoy
my self-employed freedom a lot!! I mostly get inspired
by the material itself or by taking a closer look at daily
objects. The teabag, for example, is exactly the same as
the one you put in your cup of hot water, but I made it
on a larger scale so you can use it as a tote bag."

The items featured were selected from the over **500,000 handmade goods** for sale on Ets
Find any of the items shown for sale, each in their own shops. Go to: shopname.etsy.com

Find the Unique. Support the Independent. Buy Handmade.

Marketplace

wish you were here?
sign up at www.etsy.com

Paper Goods
epositive $3

Jewelry
squrlgurl $259.75

Books & Zines
Kreativlink $35

Clothing
lebouton $38

Art
belleandboo $20

Knitting
inessa $12.50

Bath & Beauty
karenssoaps $3.75

Bags & Purses
zakiyaa $45

Children
quiltbaby $15

Plants & Edibles
Marmalady $4.50

Ceramics & Pottery
misslo $55

Toys
huddle $15

Accessories
KitMit $6.50

Music
intothefire $7.50

Woodworking
stumppondtoy $20.75

Jewelry
esdesigns $19

Etsy seller: matteart

"The first thing I can specifically remember working on was in kindergarten. Everyone had to do a posterboard painting about their favorite part of the *Wizard of Oz*. I remember working on it with my dad and the great feeling it gives you when you finish something you like. I still try to get that same feeling out of my work."

Make things? Join the community of over 60,000 individual artists, artisans, crafters, and makers of all things handmade who are selling their goods on Etsy. It doesn't matter what you make, as long as you do it yourself.

Your place to buy and sell all things handmade. Etsy.com

From Grocery Cart to Crafted Art

Sturdy, clanking, and common — these are words that describe your typical grocery cart, but when it comes to artist **Crystal Schenk**'s stained glass sculpture, the words fragile, beautiful, and extraordinary are more like it.

Of all things to adorn with stained glass, why a grocery cart? "I like to work with materials that have their own built-in significance and histories," says Schenk, who remodels homes part time. She was inspired on the job, in upscale houses using high-end materials including stained glass, and then returning home, where "homeless people walk through the neighborhoods with shopping carts, collecting cans and bottles to return for deposit money." The contrast between these two "lifestyles" made a lasting impression on Schenk.

A 30-year-old MFA student at Portland State University, Schenk spent three months on the fully functional cart, which she calls *Have and Have Not*. "I really enjoyed taking a commonplace object that is often overlooked, and turning it into something extraordinary that couldn't be ignored."

Extraordinary indeed.

—*Carla Sinclair*

Photograph by Crystal Schenk